Memories of
SOUTHERN
Railways

Mike Jacobs

© Noodle Books and Mike Jacobs 2011   ISBN 978-1-906419-64-6

First published in 2011 by Kevin Robertson under the **NOODLE BOOKS** imprint
PO Box 279 Corhampton, SOUTHAMPTON SO32 3ZX

www.noodlebooks.co.uk

Printed in England by Ian Allan Publishing Ltd.

INTRODUCTION

I had been toying with setting down some memories of Southern lines in my earlier life for some time, and was encouraged to turn thoughts into reality by the publisher, Kevin Robertson. I have tried very hard to maintain as much accuracy as possible, and in this I have from time to time been assisted by others who have been kind enough to clarify my first thoughts. I am greatly indebted to them for their assistance and to Kevin for his ever-present and sustaining enthusiasm. I must also mention the great help that I received from an old friend of mine, Ed McNeil, who vetted the text word by word, and who prevented me from going down too many grammatical and syntactical dead-ends, in spite of the fact that when he started out on the mission he had little interest in railways, a state of affairs which I am delighted to say has now changed more than somewhat.

None of the illustrations, to my knowledge, has ever previously been published, and I am delighted that examples from my own archive have been added to by other images, principally from the collection of the late Denis Callender, reproduced with the kind permission of his son, Jonny.

In producing this work I have dug deep into the mine of recollection, and I hope that the finished book might entertain the reader as much as I was entertained in its writing.

Mike Jacobs
Fleurance
Gers
France

August 2011

All unaccredited views were taken by the Author.

Front cover, top - *Wheel delivery at Brighton Works. 'E4' No. 32481 propelling three wagons of locomotive wheels. 12 April 1957.*

Front cover, bottom - *DS1169, the resident shunter at Broad Clyst permanent way depot. 8 August 1964. See pages 60/69.*

Rear cover - *Boilers at the rear of Eastleigh Works, 16 April 1958. Those on view include, 'LN', MN', 'WC', 'T9', 'M7' and 'Standard Class 4' types.*

Frontispiece - *Battle of Britain No. 34063 '229 Squadron' leaving Waterloo with a Basingstoke and Salisbury train, 27 February 1964..*

Opposite page - *Seaton Junction, 13 June 1964. 'N' class 2-6-0 No. 31859 arriving with the 16.40 all-stations to Exeter Central.*

Above - *An unidentified 'D15' 4-4-0 backing out of Platform 5 at Portsmouth and Southsea, no doubt bound for the depot at Fratton, April 1949. The lines to the High Level station and Portsmouth Harbour are on the extreme right.*

Denis Callender

Left - *The entrance to Portsmouth and Southsea after the enemy raid of 9.00 pm on 3/4 May 1941. Officially this was reported as a 'fairly minor' event, notwithstanding the explosion of a delayed action bomb under an electric unit at the station - one coach was blown in half and another badly damaged. The station was reopened after 15 hours.*

RCHS Spence collection

Prologue

Can it be common that a first memory is of a sound not an image? This is surely the case, however, with my first remembered brush with railways, which early on became an abiding passion in my life. My family lived in Earlsfield in south west London in 1943, and we were within a reasonably short walk of Wandsworth Common. The Common is bisected by the old London, Brighton and South Coast Railway's main line, and I am told that on family walks my brother and I insisted on spending time here watching the trains. I remember nothing of all this visually, but have a unshakeable memory of the ponderous and resonating 'bong, bong, bong, bong' of freight train wheels on jointed track, and the clang of buffers as loose couplings stretched and slackened with the train's progress. These sounds have all but gone now, but they were once the audible evidence of railways going about much of their business, and clearly they made an indelible impression upon me.

My first visual memory, as it were, of railways is one of a year or so later, and concerns territory located many miles to the west of Wandsworth. We lived for a few months near the village of Edington, in the Polden Hills between Bridgwater and Glastonbury in Somerset. This was in the kingdom of the Somerset and Dorset Joint Railway, and so qualifies for inclusion as a Southern recollection. These were stirring times, and our residence spanned the period two or three months before and after the D-Day landings. Aside from anything to do with railways, I can remember Double Summer Time, vigorous agricultural activity and practice flights overhead by aircraft towing the gliders that were to be used in the invasion. Sometime during the summer the family took a day trip to the nearest seaside town, the small resort of Burnham-on-Sea, which is to be found squatting between a sandy beach - or is it estuary mud? - and the edge of the Somerset levels which verge the Bristol Channel at this point.

In those days our station was called 'Edington Junction' and was where the Bridgwater branch, even then declining, but with war-time traffic which stayed its execution for a while, detached itself from the main line at Evercreech Junction.

I know that we walked the mile or so to the station where we parked my sister's pram, to be collected on our return, before catching the train which pottered the few miles more to Burnham, but I cannot recall its passage. I do, however, recall waiting on the platform for the return journey. The single platform at Burnham seemed very long and was partly protected by an overall roof, and the train was hauled by a black locomotive. There is one other railway associated memory of the day. On our return to Edington Junction there was some parental dismay and wrath, because my sister's pram' had somehow been allowed to fall on to the track and had been damaged. I have a belief that no parental satisfaction was obtained in the matter.

We moved on before too long. My father was appointed to a post in the Naval Dockyard at Portsmouth, took up residence in Southsea, and we left Somerset for Hampshire to join him in late 1944. The number of changes of train *en route* stay in my mind, probably due to the encumbrance of luggage and that pram'.

Looking back, we must have left and joined trains at Evercreech Junction, Templecombe and Salisbury. There is a memory of a 'Merchant Navy' bringing a train into a station, which must have been Templecombe, and behind which we must have travelled to Salisbury. It was in Southern wartime black livery, and seemed massive – hardly like a locomotive at all.

Portsmouth introduced me to the Southern Electric, which I honestly found a bit boring, although representing the box-like trains in childish drawings inadvertently led me to discover how to draw things in perspective. From time to time father had to travel to London and I accompanied my mother to meet him on his return either to Portsmouth and Southsea or to Portsmouth Harbour stations. I preferred the former because there was the odd steam locomotive to be seen. Nowadays a shadow of its former self on the lower level, I remember it as a rather grand place, nobly recovering from earlier bomb damage, with a wide concourse, five terminal and two elevated platforms, the latter dealing with through traffic to and from Portsmouth Harbour, and with a dark and noisome gents' toilet. It was at Portsmouth and Southsea that I had my first visit to a locomotive footplate. This took place at the north side of the station, and didn't feature a Southern locomotive at all, but a GWR specimen, a member of the 'Hall' class, I think. It must have come in on a train from Cardiff or Reading, and I was delighted at being able to get close to it. One of the footplate men asked if I wanted to visit and helped me up, and I gazed about me with wide-eyed fascination, especially at the furious flames and white-hot coals viewed through the open firebox door.

The Harbour Station was less exciting, but always busy. It too, was recovering from the attentions of the *Luftwaffe*, and the former Watering Island branch to the Dockyard's South

5

Portsmouth & Southsea in the late 1940s. A member of the 'L12' class, possibly No. 30420 ,awaiting departure with a Salisbury, via Redbridge (Southampton) service. The Western Region engine alongside, No. 5956 'Horsley Hall', is probably heading a train for Reading.   *Denis Callender*

'K10' 4-4-0 No. 142 makes a spirited departure from Portsmouth Harbour, circa 1948.   *Denis Callender*

Railway Jetty was out of commission, never to reopen, and soon to have its track removed. A noteworthy memory here concerned my first sighting of a banana. A sailor, clearly returning from warmer climes, passed with a massive bunch of the fruit on his shoulder. As he boarded the 4-COR unit making up part of a train for London, I asked my mother what they were. "Bananas" she said. "What do you do with them?" I asked. "Eat them" she replied. I felt rather unsure about that.....

During the time we lived in Southsea we had a number of excursions by train, and I discovered the magical little pocket of steam which was the Hayling Island branch. There was also a visit to Southampton, which I remember more for its tramcars than as a memorable journey. We rode a tram, which I am sure was painted all-over grey and was open-topped.

These little snippets from the past make up some form of introduction, albeit a little blurred around the edges, perhaps, to the background of this abiding passion for railways; the next phase of my life produces some sharper and more de-tailed images.

The disused spur, known as the Watering Island branch from Portsmouth Harbour station to the Dockyard's South railway Jetty. Damaged during the war, and subsequently disused, these pictures show the trackless portion towards the Dockyard, and the track being lifted at the Harbour station end.

Denis Callender

M7s in south Hampshire, around 1950. **Top** *is No. 54 at Fareham and* **bottom** *entering Cosham with what is probably the Portsmouth portion of a through service to Brighton. At Fareham a member of the class might be seen on any one of a number of duties, the Fareham - Portsmouth portion of through services or working either the Gosport or Meon Valley trains.*

Both: Denis Callender

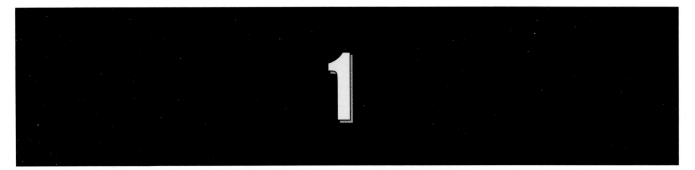

The end of the second war and the subsequent settling of the dust, meant that some semblance to the normality which was remembered by those alive before the conflict was reinstated, even if gradually and rather slowly in many respects. As a war baby who had known only wartime conditions, I sometimes found the whole business of the gradual transition to peacetime life a little odd, because the reversion to the claimed paradise of the previous order seemed to be a long time in coming. Whilst we all waited for things to change radically, I think that a helpful connection to my established normality was the constancy of railways. They were always there and could always be relied upon to yield some interest. As a by-product of the peace, the little Southsea Miniature Railway which had closed for the duration of the war, reopened. It was not too far from where we lived at the time, and provided a pleasant focus for family walks, into which a ride on the 10¼ inch gauge line was sometimes incorporated.

Father left the Admiralty, and in common with a respectable percentage of the population of Portsea Island who needed re-housing, we moved in 1947 to a new rapidly developing Corporation housing estate which was in the process of laying waste to a half-mile wide swathe of land between the north end of Portsmouth Harbour and the lower slopes of Portsdown Hill. This estate was the, now somewhat infamous in parts, settlement known as Paulsgrove. The busy tracks of the Portsmouth to Southampton and Eastleigh railway informally marked the southern boundary between the estate and the rest of the world.

In spite of the rapid rise in population of the territory, there was no railway station to serve the settlement, although there were the remains of platforms built from old sleepers which had formed a stopping place designated as 'Paulsgrove Halt' prior to the outbreak of war. It was opened to serve a racecourse at the foot of Portsdown Hill, and died when horses ceased to run in 1939. The remains of the racecourse were already submerged beneath the acres of roads and council houses when we arrived. Our residence here lasted for over four years – plenty of time to get to know the area's railways intimately.

The nearest extant station was Cosham, and I spent many hours over the years I was close by watching trains through the railings protecting the east-bound platform. It may not have been the most exciting of places, but there was a good train service – around thirty a day in each direction stopped there – and plenty of variety in locomotive types. Former London and South Western Railway 4-4-0s featured strongly, and I particularly remember the T9s, but my still extant, if somewhat dog-eared and yellowing, copy of the 1948 Ian Allan ABC of Southern Locomotives reminds me that there were S11s, D15s, L11s and L12s also. In the ABC, too, is a baffling pencilled reference to the fact that I observed a locomotive numbered 624, which was not listed in the book, but was in the series allotted to the LSW A12

Southampton Road at Paulsgrove. The board at the rear of the pantechnican states, "Filming in progress, please slow down". What was the film, I wonder?
        Denis Callender

0-4-2s, a few of which were still around in those days. No. 624 was withdrawn in 1947, several months before I started to note down numbers. Curious, this; I wonder if I saw it on its way to Eastleigh for demolition, or was this merely a mistaken childhood observation?

There were also frequent appearances by M7 0-4-4Ts and 700 Class 0-6-0s. Ex-LBSCR types were to be seen, too. Naturally, because this was South Western territory, these were less numerous, although all the Brighton Atlantics, of both class H1 and H2, and every one of the 4-6-0s of class N15X, rebuilt from the Baltic tanks, were noted on passenger trains, presumably on through workings to and from Brighton. Southern Moguls were there, as were 'King Arthurs', Q1s and, excitingly, in small quantities 'West Country' and 'Battle of Britain' light Pacifics. 'Foreign' classes were scarcely visible, although ex-GWR types appeared on the Cardiff and Reading to Portsmouth workings, and I remember that *Cherwell Hall* (No. 4989) seemed to visit frequently.

Cosham station itself was a place of some interest. It was my first introduction to a level crossing where the gates were opened and closed by the signalman in the adjacent signal cabin spinning a large wheel. The short bars secreted in the road which raised or lowered themselves in unison with the movement of the gates and locked them when they were closed to road traffic, intrigued me. The road – Cosham High Street – was reasonably busy, but most of the through traffic used a by-pass road which I think, at its northern end, occupied part of the track-bed of the former Portsmouth and Horndean Light Railway, and which crossed the main railway to the west of the level crossing and the late light railway's girder bridge by a modern pre-cast concrete structure. Of course, at that time I knew nothing of the light railway, which was really a tramway, and which was one of the few British lines that in a rather micro-

scopic way might have been said to have vaguely resembled an American inter-urban line. It closed in January 1935, but several signs of its presence were still extant in the area. The abutments of the bridge by which it had crossed Southwick Hill Road, at the north of Cosham, were clearly visible, as were the remnants of its right of way alongside the London Road towards the top of Portsdown Hill, although I didn't know what they were in those days. At this time the Light Railway's bridge over the main line still had odd lengths of track *in situ* amongst the undergrowth occupying the line of the former tramway. I think that the bridge was finally demolished around 1953.

At this time, both Corporation and Southdown buses stopped or terminated in what I think was known as the 'Corporation Compound', a somewhat unkempt area of land adjacent to the south side of the level crossing, opposite where the City trams used to terminate, and I think that there were some discarded lengths of tram track piled on one side of the perimeter.

In the opposite direction to Cosham from where we lived the nearest station was Portchester. We used this for any trips to the west. I did not find the station desperately exciting; it merely consisted of two platforms connected by a footbridge. I recall the place as being clean and tidy, but the most memorable thing from my point of view were the notices by the ticket collector's hutches which read "All Season Tickets Must be Shewn". As a youngster who sometimes had problems with conventional spelling, this archaic form of the word 'shown' was somewhat confusing.

Portsdown Hill, which rose to a height of around 400 feet in parts, stretched behind various housing developments from the east of Cosham to the west of Portchester. It was not a bad place to get something of a bird's-eye view of the north of Portsea Island, on which Portsmouth stood, and the muddy expanse of Portsmouth Harbour into which was in-

The site of Paulsgrove Halt looking east towards Cosham on 22 April 1951. The Halt was used for race traffic only, and the race course was located on the north (left) side of the line. It opened on 28 June 1933 and closed on an unreported date in 1939.
Denis Callender

Right - The trackbed of the Portsmouth &
Horndean Light Railway, with some
lengths of rail still in position, viewed from
the Light Railway's bridge over the main
line, looking north, in the late 1940s.
Denis Callender

*Bottom - Successors to the tramcars,
Portsmouth Corporation trolleybuses wait
for business in the area known as
'Corporation Compound', adjacent to
Cosham station Their livery was maroon
and cream.*

Denis Callender

serted Whale Island and Horsea Island, in those days both
Naval outposts of the main dockyard. Towards the east end
of Portsdown one could get a distant view of electric units
scuttling between Portsmouth and Havant. Towards the
west, there were opportunities to see steam trains on the
Southampton line. In the days when I lived at Paulsgrove,
there were also interesting things to be seen in the harbour
itself. The glorious and final British battleship HMS *Van-
guard,* which never fired a gun in anger, spent much of its
later life parked there, as did the old and beautiful Royal

Yacht, the third *Victoria and Albert.*

With that immaculate lack of attention to detail which sometimes distinguishes the planning of major developments,
those who governed the Paulsgrove project showed some
excellence in the installation of prefabs and the construction
of reasonably roomy and well-built houses and the network
of roads which served them all, but seemed to have initially
completely overlooked the need for shops, public houses
and other social centres for the rapidly growing population.
Even schools were late in arriving, and it was 1949 before I

Early summer 1949 at Cosham with WD 2-8-0 No. 77270 shunting the yard.
Denis Callender

A 1949 view of the level crossing at Cosham looking towards Fareham recorded from the station footbridge. On the extreme left are a number of concrete cubes erected in WW2 and intended to inconvenience an invading enemy. Known as "Dragon's Teeth", they were designed to impede the progress of tanks. They appear very clearly in the lower photograph on page 8. Notwithstanding the fact that a number of men are working on the crossing, the home signal may be seen in the 'off' position. The actual resurfacing of the crossing involved the use of a steam-roller.
Denis Callender

began to be educated within the community in which we lived.

This was not completely bad news, however, at least for me, because in common with a fairly large number of my contemporaries I spent a year in the neighbouring primary school three quarters of a mile away on the edge of the more ancient council estate at Wymering. I say that it wasn't completely bad news because from the classroom I occupied there was a splendid view of the railway. This may not have helped too much with my concentration on educational things, spelling, for example, but it was a great boost to my abiding passion. In addition to the normal comings and goings, I particularly remember that sometime around eleven o'clock each morning a long train, usually made up of an assortment of vans of various shapes and sizes and usually double-headed, often with one of the locomotives a member of the "King Arthur" class, headed towards the west. Another reasonably frequent sight were trains of hopper wagons, mainly of the bogie variety, loaded with ballast, pre-

sumably from Meldon Quarry in Devon if heading east, or empty if west-bound. I think that these were generally hauled by an H15 or S15 class 4-6-0, and had one of the unique Southern bogie brake vans at the rear.

As is inevitably the case, those youthful days were always sunny, and this certainly applied to my favourite train-watching station, rather more distant than Cosham or Portchester, Fareham. This place was full of interest. There were four platforms, two of which served the through lines to and from Southampton and Eastleigh. On the other side of that which served trains heading east towards Portsmouth there was a bay into which at long intervals the push-pull train which served the Meon Valley line quietly sidled. At that time the Meon Valley line used a single track on the original formation of the London and Southampton Railway's branch from Bishopstoke, later Eastleigh, to Gosport. Because of uncertain earth movements, the main line to the latter place had been re-routed many years before in an arc to the south between Fareham and Knowle. Today the

Left - Porchester looking east towards Paulsgrove and Cosham. Up and down lines here were designated as 'up' for eastbound trains and 'down' for westbound.

Denis Callender

original route is again used, and the southerly arc is abandoned. The fourth platform at Fareham, the other side of the island that served trains going west, was largely used by trains on the Gosport branch. I must have spent hours over the years sitting on that island platform, in the sun, of course, watching the action unfold.

Fareham station was a location where one never had to wait too long for something to happen. There was a pretty regular local passenger service, and some interesting through trains, the doyen of which was probably the Plymouth to Brighton express. This was usually in the charge of a Bulleid Light Pacific, and its stop at Fareham was made of further interest because it detached, or attached, a through portion – two or three coaches, I think – to and from Portsmouth and Southsea. This train introduced me to the well-known slipping propensities of the Bulleid Pacifics, and I can remember some splendidly noisy and vigorous departures, particularly in the easterly direction where trains had to navigate a sharp curve, accompanied by rapidly revolving driving wheels and a sky-reaching column of exhaust. After this performance, the departure of the Portsmouth section

was much more sedate, unobtrusive even, and was, as I recall, usually in the hands of an M7.

A large goods yard was adjacent to the Meon Valley bay, and there was always the sound of loading and unloading, and on the odd occasion the attendance of the local pick-up freight. The western side was not without its goods activity, either. Outside the running lines for the Gosport trains, there was a siding which served a coal merchant, but not, as it were, directly. A length of standard gauge track which had no physical connection to the railway proper was laid between the siding and the coal staithes and was the domain of a steam crane which trundled up and down from time to time unloading coal wagons and depositing their contents in the appropriate staithe. I presume that this arrangement was the property of the coal merchant, and it always made something extra to watch.

The Gosport branch train provided me with my second footplate visit. After arrival, the locomotive and two or three coaches hovered for a time, and once during this period of relative inactivity, my brother and I were invited aboard M7

Ex LBSCR J2 4-6-2T No. 2326 near Cosham with what was reported as a "Director's Special" on 7 May 1948. The destination is unknown, but the headcode is that used between Brighton and Salisbury via Eastleigh.

Denis Callender

0-4-4T No. 30674 for a brief look round. The various controls were explained to us by the driver, whilst the fireman slaked his thirst from a lemonade bottle containing what looked like dark-coloured 'Tizer', but which was later revealed to us as cold tea. Again, I was spellbound by the experience, and was a tiny bit sad when the crew waved us a cheery farewell and the little train fussed away busily to make another visit to Gosport.

It was a shame that aside from the sidling push-pull trains at Fareham I never got to know the lovely Meon Valley line, except for a little vision encountered one day when my brother and I were seeking out ponds and streams where we could catch minnows and sticklebacks. We saw from the road between Wickham and Droxford a short train of mixed wagons heading north through the meadows, drawn by a 4-4-0, possibly of Class S11.

I have already noted that the whole of the N15X class of 4-6-0s was observed during this period. I recall them as handsome locomotives, although with later knowledge I would have loved to have seen them in their original form. My father was not a railway historian, but he could admire a fine locomotive when he saw one. He was with me when my first sighting happened, and when No. 32333 *Remembrance* was bagged, rightly opined that the name was a celebration of casualties of the Great War. Dad was a man always fascinated by maritime things, particularly if they were naval, and I'm afraid to say that my logging of my second N15X caused some nautical confusion. I reported that I had observed No. 32331 *Beattie*, and Dad immediately assumed that it was named after the Admiral who commanded the British battle-cruiser fleet at Jutland (we did not discuss spelling). When the next sighting – No. 32329 *Stephenson*, I think – came along, we had to re-think things, and light dawned on the notion that, titular head of the class aside, locomotive engineers were the order of the day.

I think that it was father's interest in things maritime that prompted our subsequent visits to Southampton, where we

went a number of times. On these trips, instead of travelling on the train into Southampton itself, we alighted to the east of the River Itchen at Woolston station, walked the short distance to the river, and crossed to the other side on the chain ferry, now long replaced by a road bridge. Technically, I suppose, it wasn't a chain ferry like the one between Portsmouth and Gosport, because it used wire cables which emerged from the water to rest on the upper part of the circumference of two pulley wheels, one fore and one aft of the

Above - 'N15X' No 32327 'Trevithick' waiting to leave Fareham on the sharp curve for Portsmouth. Straight ahead the line continues to Gosport. Late 1940s.

Denis Callender

Left - The Portsmouth portion of the through Brighton - to Plymouth service crossing the viaduct at Fareham creek in 1949. The locomotive is an oil-burning member of the 'T9' class.

Denis Callender

14

Right -
A Plymouth to Brighton service waiting to leave Fareham (the engine, No. 34040 'Crewkerne' stationary a little distance ahead of the starting signal).
Denis Callender

Bottom - In SR livery, T9 No. 116 waits at Fareham with a Portsmouth service. 2 July 1949.
Denis Callender

15

Canute Road crossing and Southampton Docks.

Top *- No. 30853 'Sir Richard Grenville' leaving the Docks with the Royal Mail Line 'Andes' boat train on 23 June 1957. This was an extra working shown as leaving at 10.45 am and arriving at Waterloo at a leisurely 12.33 pm.*

Bottom *- Another boat train, this time with no obvious identification. The engine is No. 34095 'Brentor', recorded on 1 April 1957.*

Both: Tony Molyneaux

No. 30859 'Lord Hood' preparing to run light to Eastleigh from Southampton Docks on 1 April 1957, having arrived with 'The South American' from Waterloo. The service was the 9.15 am from Waterloo, destined for the vessel 'Alcantara', the load reported as 11 vehicles including three Pullmans.

Tony Molyneaux

vessel, before they again became submerged. The powering of the pulley wheels thus drove the contraption along. After the crossing we walked a short distance south until we found ourselves on Canute Road, and here the fun really started. First, there was the main railway crossing from the vicinity of Southampton Terminus to the Ocean Liner terminal, vaguely sighted through the gates. Here, if one was lucky, could be seen the splendid Ocean Liner Expresses, usually headed by a 'Lord Nelson' or a Bulleid Pacific, cautiously crossing the road, or sometimes an express locomotive running light and equally gingerly before or after its duty on such workings.

From this point another track emerged from the Terminus tracks to run along the road towards some sidings and Town Quay, and onwards from there to connect with the tracks of the Western Docks. Walking towards Town Quay there were fleeting glimpses of parts of liners over the wall which separated the road from the nautical action, and I can remember seeing the upper works of the last four-funnelled Cunarder, the 'Aquitania', in the final phase of her life, and the 'Mauretania' in the dry dock. On our visits, most of which were in 1949, the shunting activity in the vicinity of Town Quay was in the hands of the tiny and charming C14 0-4-0Ts, but we also saw USA class 0-6-0Ts, not too long liberated from the US Army Transportation Corps post-war

dump of surplus railway items at Newbury. The latter locomotives, squat, powerful-looking and without running plates, made an instant impression on me. In common with many of the types of machines encountered in this chapter of my life, I was to meet them again several times in future years. On one trip we took the ferry which ran from Town Quay across Southampton Water to Hythe. As might be expected, it was again a sunny day, and there were good views of many vessels, including various ocean liners – Cunarders berthed in the original older docks and, amongst others alongside the Western Docks, members of the beautiful lilac-hulled Union Castle fleet. At Hythe a couple of charms awaited me. The first was the delightful Hythe Pier Railway, two-foot gauge, electrified and using curious little locomotives which I learned much later had started life in a First World War Ministry of Munitions mustard gas factory. Used to travel between the pier head and its landward end, it is happily still with us today. The second charm was discovered after we had walked through the little town, passing under the late-built and light Fawley branch, and had taken another minor road which led us back to the shoreline. We crossed an un-gated level crossing over the railway, and discovered nearby Z class 0-8-0T No. 30956 simmering patiently during a pause in shunting the long siding adjacent to and below the level of Hythe Station. Because of these two charms Hythe enjoyed thereafter a warm place in my

The Hythe Pier tramway in 1953.

Both: Denis Callender

One of the diminutive 'C14' shunters, which performed duty at Southampton Town Quay, Redbridge sleeper works and occasionally at Winchester. No. 30588 recorded near Canute Road crossing, Southampton. 20 April 1957.

Tony Molyneaux

memory, although I have not visited since and I know from hearsay that it is radically changed from those days. There was, incidentally, another charm, although not a railway one. At Hythe were accommodation and maintenance facilities for BOAC's Shorts 'Empire' flying boats, and I saw one – the 'Canopus' - moored there. On one Southampton visit we watched one of these machines take off down Southampton Water, and very impressive it was, too.

There was another trip, too, to the west, this time to Winchester. By this time I knew of the existence of Eastleigh Works, and was disappointed that not much could be seen from the train. Of Winchester I have to admit that the cathedral enthralled me more than the railway station, which is probably unfair to the railway. Clearly, I was not at the station when expresses or trains of other exciting kinds passed through.

During our residency at Paulsgrove there were journeys in the other direction, including several trips to London. Not too much remains in my mind of the latter, except the bustle and business which increased as the metropolis became closer, the long-shanked hydraulic buffers at Waterloo, and

the call button marked 'Steward' by the seats – even in the third class which we occupied – in the 4-COR electric units. On at least one trip I can remember the white-jacketed steward striding purposefully up the centre aisle urging passengers to "Take your seats for tea, please, ladies and gentlemen; take your seats for tea."

On one occasion, we went a little way up the Portsmouth Direct Railway to Petersfield, where I can remember standing on the down platform watching a London express – 4-COR, 4-RES, 4-COR – hurtle through, corridor connections at each end swaying with the speed. Of additional interest on the other side of the road bridge was the remote platform used by the infrequent push-pull to Midhurst. Closer to home we walked fairly often to Havant, crossing the main line by the level crossing at Bedhampton Halt, and once or twice again sampled the delights of the Hayling Island Branch.

Many trips were also made to the Isle of Wight and I fell completely in love with its unique and delightful railway system. I have written of these trips and my subsequent experiences in the Island elsewhere[1], and I think that revis-

1. "Memories of Isle of Wight Railways", Noodle Books 2010

Left - Once upon a time through trains used to travel in a huge number of different directions. A study in roofboard detail at Winchester in the early days of nationalisation.

Denis Callender

Bottom - Fresh from rebuilding and on a running-in turn. No. 35014 'Nederland Line' leaves Winchester for Basingstoke, 15 July 1956.

Tony Molyneaux

Seen in the evening sunlight at Eastleigh on 26 August 1950, the only 'Leader' to ever steam, No. 36001 awaits its next test working.
Denis Callender

iting them would be superfluous right now: important to me though they were, perhaps they don't really belong in this work.

As has already been remarked, shopping facilities were late in arriving in Paulsgrove, and for the length of our tenure there we used the services of a newsagent across the railway on the Southampton Road. The bridge we used to get to the shop was next to the remains of Paulsgrove Halt and has since gone, but it was a good spot to watch trains from, as were other areas of nearby territory. In those days, adjacent to the lane over the bridge and between the railway and the main road was a playing field used by pupils from St John's College, a Roman Catholic school based in the heart of Portsmouth. What the relationship was between the school and the field I don't know, but when it was not being used for sporting activities it was an excellent place into which to trespass to get close to the line. The rougher, as yet undeveloped, territory on the north side of the railway wasn't bad, either, but more uncomfortable to access. It was at this spot that I had my first and only view of the original British Railways carriage livery, carried by a solitary coach sandwiched between Southern green. This new colour scheme, which was not, I am told, dissimilar to the old London and North Western coach livery, and which was sometimes referred to as "plum and spilt milk", seemed very agreeable to me.

For the last couple of years or so of my school life in Paulsgrove a regular after school task was to collect father's newspaper and one or two other journals from the newsagent, and this gave grand opportunities for short bursts of spotting. The newspaper collection time neatly coincided

with an east-bound express working always headed by a Bulleid Light Pacific, on one or two occasions so new that no name plate was fixed. Over the years this setting became a rich lode for sightings, and even the collection of my copy of the 'Eagle', published every Friday, as proclaimed by its masthead banner, did not deter me from spending a little time here most school days. A surreptitious advance look at "Dan Dare – Pilot of the Future" could wait until I was wending my way home.

There were a couple of occasions when the minor trespassing on the St John's College field was particularly memorable. A long dirty-grey machine, which, because it had windows at the ends, looked something like the pictures I had seen of the Southern main-line electric locomotives, but with exhaust emerging from the top of the body at one end, emerged from under the bridge. Our line was not, of course, electrified in those days, so electric locomotive it couldn't be. Its progress was stately as it headed west, and the exhaust purred. "What was that?" I asked myself, wide-eyed. "That", I found out a couple of years later, was the only ever functioning member of Bulleid's 'Leader' class, No. 36001. The purring sound of the six-cylinder exhaust contributed to my lifelong interest in these machines, and stays with me still. The machine was followed after a decent interval by the appearance of a light engine, which I'm pretty sure was an E4 0-6-2T, presumably sent out to conform with what was by then the established protocol of having another locomotive handy in case the 'Leader' broke down. Some weeks later this fascinating locomotive passed by again, endorsing my curiosity. I can't pinpoint the dates of my two sightings, but thanks to the thorough research by Kevin

Robertson published in his book "The Leader Project"[2] they would have been between February and October 1950, when the locomotive made various trips between Brighton, Fratton, Cosham and Eastleigh. I have always felt a little privileged to have been able to witness at first hand, albeit briefly, the results of Bulleid's last Southern experiment.

In 1949 my brother and I acquired some tickets to a youth match at Portsmouth Football Club's ground at Fratton Park. Unlike apparently almost every other member of the human race then and now, I was not that interested in football, but going to the match was something to do on a Saturday morning. Access to the ground was by way of Goldsmith Road which passed Fratton Motive Power Depot, and the score was, therefore, "Football 0 – Railways 1". I particularly remember a line of dead locomotives, amongst which were a number converted for oil burning. I had seen one or two such as these, probably L11s or T9s, easily recognised by the box-like oil tanks standing high in their tenders, in

2. Oxford Publishing Company, 2007

action at Cosham, but I can't recall any difference in the smell of their emissions. For a time they were quite a common and unremarkable sight.

The Paulsgrove phase of my early life ended in early 1952, when we moved to north-west London. I had mixed feelings about the change. Part of me was excited by the challenge of a new life in a new place, and, doubtless, the discovery of much new interesting railway stuff. Another part was a little sad to be leaving all the Southern things which had been so much a part of life so far. Maybe it is fitting that my last railway memory of this era is of a grubby, run-down looking locomotive whose type I can't remember, heading light towards the west, perhaps on its final trip to Eastleigh for destruction. Dirty it may have been, but underneath the grime there was still malachite green, and its tender still sported the word 'Southern' in sunshine lettering.

The edge of the EMU shed at Fratton on 24 April 1958 with Goldsmith Avenue, leading to Fratton Park football ground alongside. In the siding is what is a former LSWR 'SUB' unit, converted for departmental use and numbered 91.

The London sojourn lasted two and a half years and opened my eyes to hitherto undiscovered termini and trains, some quite fascinating. I dug deep into the City of London, remotest Middlesex and Hertfordshire, and some of the darkest corners of the Underground system. In spite of all these, my liking for Southern stuff and Southern territory remained paramount. At a fairly local level, visits were made to Kew and Richmond, and I spent some thinking time trying to figure out how Southern third-rail electrics and four-rail North London Line and London Transport trains could share the same tracks, as they did, and still do, in this vicinity.

A pleasant happening, which took me back to well-trodden territory, was a holiday in the Isle of Wight in 1953. I was becoming more familiar with the Waterloo to Portsmouth Harbour run year by year. We always used the fast services which had only three intermediate stops, aside from Ports-

mouth and Southsea and, occasionally, Havant. These were at Woking, Guildford and Haslemere. As I grew up and became more observant it became clear that although these were all thoroughly "Southern" places, the communities they served were all of different flavours. Woking was busy, and clearly focused on commuters. Guildford, an important crossroads for routes in six directions, was leafy, and seemed to be where commuting territory met the country. Haslemere was quieter, even more leafy, and was clearly gentrified.

Although our trains were electrics there was still much steam to be seen. There was always plenty of activity at Waterloo; station pilots and enticing glimpses of express workings heading in the direction of Bournemouth, Weymouth and the more distant reaches of the West Country. In terms of locomotive depots, there were Nine Elms and Stewart's Lane, visible at some distance as the train acceler-

Headcode 80 indicates a Waterloo to Portsmouth Harbour via Woking service. 4-COR No. 3142 heads a COR/RES/COR formation south of Petersfield.

KR Collection

ated out of London, and then there was the roundhouse – actually, only half a roundhouse – at Guildford, and finally the depot at Fratton. And there was always the possibility of encountering steam in any of the goods yards *en route* and at the branch termini south of Guildford.

In 1954 interesting summer excursions were made to Folkestone, and a somewhat less interesting one to Eastbourne. The Folkestone trips started at Charing Cross, and on each occasion involved workings which paused at Sevenoaks, Tonbridge and Ashford, and which were always headed by members of the 'Schools' class. Sadly, I can remember little of these journeys, and nothing much of Ashford works, either. Presumably because we were to alight at Folkestone Central and were gathering up our goods and chattels and looking for the signs of the approaching station, I can remember the junction with the then defunct line to Hythe, the Kentish version this time, with no narrow gauge railway on a pier, but with the much more famous narrow-gauge line to Dungeness. Try as I might, I could not get the family itinerary of these visits altered to accommodate a visit to this wonder.

I can't remember much about Folkestone Central, but I do recall a train running through the station with some of its coaches sporting the numeral '2' on their doors. By this time I knew enough about railway history to know that second class had disappeared long before so I found this a bit odd, and it wasn't until a few years afterwards that I found out that second class accommodation was still offered on some trains to cater for those who had booked this standard on journeys from France, where second was still present.

Folkestone in those days still retained something of the Edwardian atmosphere heart-achingly conveyed by H G Wells' 1905 novel 'Kipps', and was a lively place. The interesting cliff railway, which well pre-dated Kipps's adventures and misadventures, and which connected the Leas with the road paralleling the sea, was (and is today) still extant, and busy. At the time of my visits Folkestone Harbour was still a busy cross channel port, and ferry sailings were served by boat trains routed over the branch which descended steeply from Folkestone Junction. Of the ferries, I particularly remember the MV *Côte D'Azur,* which looked smart and modern, and whose name gave an appetising flavour of things alluringly French (even if it only sailed as far as Boulogne!). I was pleased when the name was perpetrated by a more recent craft built in 1981[3].

The trains descended from the main line quietly and sedately, but the ascending workings were a totally different kettle of fish, and were superb to behold and hear. Restrictions prevented the use of main line locomotives, and during the time of my visits all workings were in the hands of ex-SECR R1 class 0-6-0Ts. The weight of ascending trains required more than one of these rather small engines, and I noted various marshalling formations, from one leading and one banking, one or two leading with one or two banking, through to the most noisy and spectacular combination of all, two at the front and two at the rear. The opportunity for trains to sprint to the foot of the incline was very limited because of the confines of the harbour, and the short distance before the ascent began. This meant that the hard work started almost immediately, and the vociferous and measured clamour of the trains towards the Junction was audible for the duration of their entire uphill journey.

On these excursions our navigation of Folkestone seemed to become almost circular. The usually adopted route, with appropriate pauses and detours for refreshment and sightseeing, was Central Station, town, the Leas, cliff railway, seafront, harbour and finally a stroll back to the Junction Station. Here we caught the train back to London, always hauled by a Standard Class 4 2-6-4T, which ran briskly through the gathering darkness to Charing Cross.

I have already intimated that I found the trip to Eastbourne pretty unexciting. This implies no intentional slur on the town, of which, frankly, I can remember little, but rather reflects the fact that the railway journey had little impact on me. The trip was accomplished by Southern Electric, efficient as ever, but unremarkable. Only two things stay with me. One of them, for some reason I cannot fathom, was my parents pointing out the disused racecourse at Gatwick as we ran through the derelict station (if they could see the place now.....!), and the other was the discovery of the 6-PUL electric units. Until then, I had assumed that all multiple units had fixed formations of green coaches, so this caused something of a rethink.

This period of my life drew to a close when we moved from London to the Isle of Wight in the autumn of 1954. From here on my fixation with railways became even more of an obsession, fuelled very much by the delights of the Island's system.

Proof that not all Southern electric units consisted solely of green coaches.   *David Hammersley Collection*

3. Perhaps it was a pity that this vessel was more prosaically renamed "SeaFrance Renoir" in 1990.

Top - *Looking back towards the station at Brighton from the North, probably in the late 1940s.*   K R Collection

SUNDAY, 29th JULY

No. 106—Train Alterations and Additions

Time	From	To	Remarks	Service No.
a.m. 4 20 (Freight)	Brighton	Eastleigh Yard	Depart Knowle Jct. 11.4 a.m. and run 19 minutes later thence.	
9 30	Bristol	Wool	**Additional.** Train No. 29.S.9. (Convey approximately 280 Gloucester A.C.F.).	109
9 40	Cheltenham	Wool	**Additional.** Train No. 29.S.76. (Convey approximately 360 Gloucester A.C.F.).	110
10 30	Weymouth	Waterloo	**Additional.** Train No. 29.S.2. (Convey approximately 260 Territorials for Waterloo and beyond).	116
10 30	Portsmouth Hbr.	Bulford Camp Sdgs.	**Additional.** Train No. 29.S.6. (Hampshire A.C.F.)	114

No. 141—10.30 a.m. Portsmouth Harbour to Bulford. Portsmouth Harbour to reserve from the front of train for the following parties of cadets.

Number of Officers and Cadets	Travelling from	Joining special train at
2 Officers, 55 Cadets	Cowes	Portsmouth Harbour
12 Officers, 122 Cadets	—	Portsmouth Harbour
22 Officers, 133 Cadets	—	Fareham
1 Officer, 33 Cadets	—	Eastleigh
1 Officer, 18 Cadets	—	Romsey

Portsmouth Harbour	..	10 30
Portsmouth & S'sea	10 34	
Fratton	10 36	
Portcreek Jct.	10 41	
Cosham	10 45	
Fareham	10 57	11 10
Eastleigh	11 32	11 37
Romsey	11 55	12 4
Kimbridge Jct.	12 10	
Mottisfont	12F12	12 17
Andover Jct.	**12 47**	**12 52**
Winchester Jct.	..	..
Worting	..	..
		D N
Basingstoke	..	..
Willesden Jct.	..	..
Rugby	..	..
Bulford C. Sidings	1 48	..
Waterloo		

Being happily anchored in the Isle of Wight for five years by no means stopped my continuing acquaintance with the mainland system. In fact, during the five years I had some very interesting excursions, and these form the background for this next set of reminiscences.

My brother had joined the Royal Engineers in the summer of 1954, and we attended his passing out ceremony in the October of that year. He was stationed in one of the multitude of camps which existed at that time in the Aldershot area, and I think that we travelled to North Camp on the outward journey, and returned from Ash Vale station later in the day. The longest leg of the journey, as ever, was made from Portsmouth Harbour to Guildford in a 4-COR electric. I remember that the journey north-west of Guildford seemed full of signs of the military, albeit with some of the sidings much more overgrown that they must have been during the war. The train, through from Redhill to Guildford and onwards to Reading, was hauled in both directions by a Southern 'Mogul' and was made up of Maunsell corridor coaches in the standard BR livery of red and cream.

A lot of Guildford shed was frustratingly out of sight from the platforms, and sharp eyes were required to see what was around from trains entering or leaving the station. Although I passed through Guildford several times in the early to mid 1950s, it was a constant disappointment that No. 30458 *Ironside* remained invisible to me. This little Hawthorn Leslie 0-4-0ST, inherited by the LSWR from the Southampton Docks Co., was the shed pilot here for many years until 1954, when she was withdrawn, and replaced by a B4 0-4-0T. What made my disappointment a little worse was that I had a like-minded school-friend who claimed with some superiority that every time *he* went through Guildford *Ironside* was clearly visible.

1955 saw a few trips away from the Island, most with no great mainland railway significance, but what was significant was that Sandown Grammar School, which I attended, had a flourishing Railway Club, nurtured by two masters who had a genuine love of railways, fostered in one gentleman because he was born and bred in the Isle of Wight and had grown up with its charming system, and in the other by his long-standing residence in the Island. A tradition of the Club was that it had occasional outings to places of railway interest, particularly ones which involved steam locomotives, and the high spot of 1955 was a winter visit to Brighton Works. A party of around twenty-five boys from our co-educational school (and they *were* all boys – sadly, we never had any girl members) set sail from Ryde on a damp

and overcast December 15, and journeyed east from Portsmouth along the Southern's line serving the Hampshire and West Sussex coastal belt to Brighton in a four coach train made up of either 2-BIL or 2-HAL units.

Quite how we got from the station to the works, I cannot recall, but I can remember clearly the first sight which met us after we had entered at the east end. To my pure delight, and doubtless that of most of my youthful companions, I was confronted with the Works Pilot, A1X No. DS377, hissing gently, and with her restored LB&SCR Stroudley livery positively gleaming in spite of the weather.

This was my first visit to a major engineering plant, and I gladly immersed myself in the unfamiliar and exciting sights and smells and sounds. Star of the show, nearly complete and half-painted in the erecting shop, was brand new Standard Class 4 2-6-4T No. 80130. The member of staff showing us around gave us a brief impromptu lecture on boiler construction and function, using a piece of chalk, which he produced from his pocket like a magician producing a rabbit from a hat, to draw diagrams on the plates of an unclad and unidentified firebox. The poor fellow, besieged by youngsters asking what must have sometimes seemed rather silly, but well-meant questions, tolerated us kindly, and, as with so many railwaymen that I met in that era, gave us generously of his time and patience.

As well as the Railway Club, Sandown School also boasted its own Army Cadet Corps, which I joined in 1955 for a couple of years. Learning bits about soldiering at the local barracks, unoccupied save for a caretaker, which featured heating stoves dating from the days of William IV, and crawling around the local golf course on 'manoeuvres' bore, I suspect, more similarity to 'Dad's Army' than to genuine military life, but the annual one-week camp got a little closer to the real thing. In 1956 the camp took place at Bulford, which was in one of those enclaves of Army activity in the neighbourhood of Salisbury Plain, and all the Isle of Wight's Cadet Corps had a special train from Portsmouth Harbour, which gathered up other Corps from South Hampshire on its way to Wiltshire. The Special Traffic Notice giving details of the working is reproduced opposite and shows the number of officers and cadets expected to board at the various stops. Incidentally, if the ratio of officers to cadets joining at a couple of the stations seems to be reminiscent an army from a banana republic, I think that I am right in remembering that a number of cadets' mothers were co-opted from two of the corps to assist with the catering at the camp, and I suspect that they counted as officers.

'L' Class 4-4-0 No. 31771 leaving Brighton on 12 April 1957 with a train for Tonbridge, via Eridge.

No. 34065 at Southampton Central, 29 September 1965. "Want to buy her? It'll cost you £30,000!"

The outward journey used the delightful, long-lost line from Mottisfont to Andover Junction, and thence to Bulford Camp by way of the normally freight only branch from Amesbury Junction. After a week of being told what a fine life the Army offered, eating food which, in spite of the best

efforts of the co-opted mothers, made school dinners seem like the stuff rumoured to be served at the Ritz, crawling around the countryside pretending to do battle with other cadets using thunder-flashes and blank .303 rounds, and watching tanks and various other pieces of military hardware in action, we boarded the train back to our native territory. Interestingly, I think that the return trip was made from Tidworth, the terminus of the ex-Midland and South Western branch from Ludgershall which was at that time, I think, the responsibility of the War Department. From there we travelled the then still extant M&SW main line to Red Post Junction and on to the LSWR main line, returning to Portsmouth Harbour again via Andover Junction and Mottisfont. Alas, I have few recollections of either the outward or return journey, but I do remember that, as with the earlier visit to the Aldershot area, there was evidence of much military railway activity in the area of the camp.

1956 also saw my renewal of acquaintance with Southampton, in the company of a school friend (the one who boasted of his sightings of *Ironside*). It was a great comfort to see a C14 again on duty at Town Quay, on this occasion no. 30589, and to find express engines still gently crossing Canute Road. We spent time at Central Station, where there was plenty of activity, and we had a good natter with the fireman of Bulleid 'Battle of Britain' Light Pacific No. 34065 *Hurricane*, prompted by our close inspection of his steed.

"Want to buy her?" he asked jovially. "It'll cost you £30,000!"

I have a feeling that this was not an entirely accurate reflection of the true cost, which might have been somewhat less, but it still seemed an immense sum of money. After all, our house was only worth about £2,500!

Later in the day we spent some time at St Denys, where the line from Portsmouth joined the London main line. Again, there was some good train watching, T9s and the like, with

Another inter-regional working, recorded Fareham bound at Cosham in the early 1950s, this time the engine is a member of the 'L' class, No. 31778. Above the first coach is the bridge which carried the former Portsmouth and Horndean Light Railway.

Denis Callender

C14 30589 creating something of a spectacle as it raced towards its home shed at Eastleigh at the end of its days work, exhaust beating quickly, diminutive three-foot driving wheels spinning rapidly, and motion flailing. One almost got out of breath just watching her.

There were other trips that year, principally to London, and the usual interesting things were to be observed *en route* and around the capital. About this time I began to get a feel for commuting, which was a very observable way of life when we travelled to the metropolis. From Portsmouth there were smart business people and naval types, the latter often in uniform. In the outer suburbs the bowler hat, seldom seen today, became a commonplace symbol of perhaps "something in the City" or senior civil servant. And all around, inside and outside Waterloo, there were hurrying hordes of more ordinary, largely un-smiling and sometimes pasty-faced, humans going about their business. Our fast trains to and from London veered towards catering for the smart business and naval types, and the bowler hats.

I think that the first trip to the mainland in 1957 was an April family outing to Brighton, whose purpose eludes me, but I think I spent much of my time there at the station. There was lots of Southern electric activity, including the departure of a 'Brighton Belle' working to Victoria. The diet of electrics was somewhat leavened by odd steam workings to un-electrified destinations, and other odd movements, including bustling E4 0-6-2T No. 32481 propelling three open wagons, loaded with locomotive driving wheels, from the London end to the sea end of the works. (See the upper picture on the front cover.)

A few days later there was a renewal of my acquaintance with Hayling Island and its branch line from Havant. A somewhat exciting prelude to the Hayling branch was provided by the sight, just west of Fratton, of E1 class 0-6-0T No. 32139 stationary, with a gentle plume of steam emerging from her safety valve, at the head of a goods train destined for Portsmouth Dockyard. One wagon in the train had derailed and dislodged the electric conductor rail, but there was no interruption to passenger service. Incidentally, I haven't yet mentioned the Dockyard branch, which connected with the up line at the high level Platform, thus requiring trains destined for the Dockyard to run "wrong line" for some distance. A short distance after the junction there was a notice which announced in no uncertain terms 'BR MAINTENANCE ENDS HERE'. It was almost as though the phrase "so watch it!" should have been added. The Dockyard branch had its own right of way for about a quar-

Left - *The Hayling Island branch in Southern days. 'A1X' No. 2655 recorded south of Langstone.*

Denis Callender

Bottom - *The Hayling Island branch in BR days: regular performer, and one of my favourites, No. 32646, awaiting the right away for Havant.*
9 April 1959.

A deserted Gosport - except for freight, late 1940s.   *Denis Callender*

ter of a mile, crossing a couple of roads on the level to thread its way into Admiralty territory by way of Unicorn Gate. One of the level crossings was guarded by a curious and apparently ancient signal which had a slotted lattice-girder post and two solid wooden arms, one for each direction, painted red on the front and white on the back.

That day the Hayling branch train was being looked after by the ex-LB&SCR, ex-LSWR, ex-FYNR, ex-SR "Terrier" no. 32646 wearing the compulsory spark arrester, necessary to protect the timber bridge which connected the island to the mainland. She afforded me my first and only ride in a mixed train. At departure time on the return journey, she drew the two coach train gently from the platform, and then reversed into the goods yard to gather up an open wagon before heading off to Havant. I remember that the wagon was in the bauxite livery carried by freight stock fitted with continuous brakes. When we arrived at Havant No. 32646 spent an interesting few minutes taking the wagon over to the goods yard panting fussily up and down as she crossed and re-crossed the main lines.

Going back to the locomotive's pedigree, in a pedantic kind of way I was pleased when I later found out that the members of the A1X class which spent time away from the mainland Southern Railway, with other owners or working in the Isle of Wight, were given back their old LB&SCR numbers, with suitably updated numerical prefixes, when they returned to the fold. Thus *Newington*, as this engine was originally named, started life as LB&SC No. 46, later no. 646, became in turn LSWR No. 734, FY&NR No. 2, Southern (Isle of Wight) W2 then W8, and then turned into

32646 upon its return to the mainland in 1949. This, of course, was not its final number. It reverted to 46 again whilst it was a static exhibit outside the "Hayling Billy" public house in Hayling Island, and is now wearing W8 once more as part of the fleet of the Isle of Wight Steam Railway.

My return to the Hayling Island branch confirmed that it was still a delight as a small railway, and I loved riding it again.

April 1957 was a busy month for my mainland railway activity, and towards the end of the month I was able to revisit my old stamping ground at Fareham. On the way there I committed a *faux pas*, quite unforgivable in someone who prided themselves in their knowledge of railways. I decided that after disembarking from the Isle of Wight ferry, I would take one of the little ferries which constantly bustled between Portsmouth and Gosport, and make my way to Gosport station, there to take the branch train to Fareham.

I duly crossed the little strip of water and found my way to the station at Gosport. It seemed rather run down, and there were no visible signs directing intending passengers. Eventually, I found my way in, and although there were some freight stock and utility vans present, there was no sign of the branch train. I tracked down a member of staff, who looked surprised at my being there. "Can you tell me the time of the next train to Fareham?" I asked innocently. His surprise turned to amusement as he replied "You'll have a long wait, sir. The last passenger train ran in 1953!" I thanked him, and crept off quietly to find one of those curi-

Interloper at Southampton Terminus. No. 3440 'City of Truro' arrives with the 12.42 pm from Didcot on 31 July 1957. Inter-regional rivalry still applied even a decade after nationalisation as the return working for the engine was on the 4.57 pm from Southampton Terminus which would stopped at Eastleigh to collect men from the SR works.....

ously "off-turquoise" coloured "Provincial" 'buses to take me to Fareham instead.

When I eventually got there, Fareham station was much as I remembered. A good procession of trains, still only steam locomotives visible, and I think the only change which registered was the fact that there was now a gantry in the goods yard to off-load containers. At the end of my session there, I took the more logical route back to Portsmouth Harbour - by rail.

The Royal Navy was still a great power at Portsmouth, and sometime during the summer term some of my school year was invited by the powers that be to visit the Naval Dockyard. Although part of the visit was something of a sightseeing tour, its main objective was to advertise the Navy as a potential employer to those who might be thinking about leaving school over the next year or two. So although we had a conducted tour of Nelson's *Victory*, the main thrust of the day was a trip around the Dockyard proper, and visits to HMS *Dolphin*, home of the RN's Submarine Service, at

Gosport, and to HMS *Vernon*, adjacent to the Harbour station, headquarters of the RN's Torpedo Branch.

Until then I had no idea of the extent of the internal rail system within the Dockyard, and, as ever on trips intended for other purposes, focused upon the railway rather more than the main feature, which, to be fair, covered a lot of other interesting stuff. I was delighted with the little shunting locomotives I saw, all with prominent spark arrestors, and some with great square dumb buffers. The Chief Petty Officer who was showing our party around eyed me rather less than enthusiastically when I asked what the initials "SNSO" painted on internal user wagons meant, and informed me somewhat snootily that they stood for 'Superintending Naval Stores Officer', and what did I want to know that for? There was a steeply graded line running down from the south side of the Harbour station in the direction of HMS *Vernon*, and I was looking forward to finding that it led to another network of lines serving this establishment. It turned out, however, that it only provided a rail connection to Gunwharf, an adjacent Army enclave, and although close by, *Vernon* did not enjoy a rail connection. At the time of my visit to I think that this spur was pretty much unused, although I do remember seeing a couple of oil tank wagons standing at its Harbour end sometime in the nineteen fifties[4]. Aside from the submarines, my interest was aroused at HMS *Dolphin* by the remains of a narrow gauge railway, with an apparently quite complicated layout, embedded in the quays. I decided not to ask our guide if he knew anything of its provenance.

Towards the end of July I made another trip to Southampton. A C14 was again at Town Quay, but not the previously observed No. 30589 which had been withdrawn the previous month. I assume that in the normal course of events it would have been replaced by its still extant sister No. 30588, but this time the other member of the class, service locomotive No. 77s, was on duty. 77s's usual place of work was at Redbridge Sleeper Depot, just to the west of Southampton. Perhaps it was standing in temporarily whilst 30588 received attention of some sort. All else was much as when I last visited, except for one thing. 1957 was the year that record-breaking GWR No. 3440 *City of Truro* was put back into running order by the Western Region to be available for special trains. Whilst not being used for these, the locomotive, which was allocated to Didcot shed, was used in revenue earning service, and handled a daily return service on the Didcot, Newbury and Southampton line. I was fortunate enough to be at Southampton Terminus when the immaculate 4-4-0 arrived with her train from the DN&S, and a fine sight she was. Oh, how one longed for the pre-grouping days when legend had it that all locomotives were turned out like this.

That year the Army Cadet Force camp took place at Lulworth in Dorset. We travelled from Yarmouth to Lymington, where I think that we took the ordinary branch train to Brockenhurst. From there we joined a special working to Wool, by-passing Bournemouth by way of 'Castleman's

4. Thanks are due to Alastair Wilson for clarifying the rail arrangements at HMS Vernon and Gunwharf.

Corkscrew' via Ringwood. That is all of this recollection, I'm afraid. As with the previous year's Army expedition, I can recall little of the journey.

My final mainland railway memory of 1957 is again associated with a school activity. In November a large party of Isle of Wight adolescents, of whom I was one, paid a visit to the Royal Shakespeare Theatre at Stratford-on-Avon. The play was 'Cymbeline', featuring Dame Peggy Ashcroft, and an enjoyable production the matinee turned out to be. Just as enjoyable for me, though, was the rail journey, again by special train, from Portsmouth Harbour. I think that there must have been several schools making the visit because I recorded the train, which had been brought up to the Harbour station by a Fratton E4 0-6-2T, as consisting of ten coaches in Southern green, including a buffet car, and our party on its own could not have occupied all that accommodation. The route was by way of Eastleigh, Winchester and Basingstoke, where we changed engines prior to entering Western territory, passing Reading on the west curve, through Oxford and on to the main line to Worcester, reaching Stratford via the now vanished line through Long Marston which approached the town from the south. We changed engines at Basingstoke again on the return journey. On the Southern portions of our trip the locomotive which handled our train was an S15. If it may be referred to in a memoir dealing principally with Southern things, perhaps I can be forgiven for mentioning that on the ex-GWR legs of our journey I remember that we passed through Adlestrop station, renowned setting for one of the most famous and evocative poems featuring the railway ever written[5]. For some reason on the outward journey our train slowed here, and although it was wintertime, it was not difficult to imagine this wayside station in the heat of summer, with all the birds of Oxfordshire and Gloucestershire singing.....

5 "Adlestrop", written in 1914 by Edward Thomas (1878-1917)

A clean example of a 'U' class 2-6-0 No. 31804 leaving Portsmouth & Southsea with a train for the Western Region - possibly a Cardiff service. 26 June 1958.

Above - Inside the Eastleigh erecting shop on 25 June 1958. Two N15s are present, the nearest being No. 30789 'Sir Guy', receiving its last ever overhaul. the background is 700 class 0-6-0 No. 30306. 25 June 1958.

Right - On my earlier visit to Eastleigh on 16 April 1958 there was to be no further use for this spare boiler for the Brighton H2 'Atlantics'.

The time of my life was approaching when I had to start thinking about job possibilities. I have already touched upon the Army's and the Navy's efforts to interest me in a life in uniform, but I knew in my heart that it was not for me. I really wanted something connected with railways, but wasn't sure what to head for. In those days, careers advice at school was extremely limited. After 'O' level examinations had been taken, I remember a brief interview, in what was virtually a broom cupboard (the school was short of space), with some sort of adviser, and a conversation which went something like:

Some Sort of Adviser: "So what are you good at?"
Me: "Well....Art".
SSoA: "Not much of a living in that. What are you interested in?"
Me: "I'm quite interested in railway engineering."
SSoA: "How's your Maths?"
Me: "Not that good, I'm afraid."
SSoA: "Hm. That won't get you far in engineering. Anyway, here's a leaflet about it."

And that, Dear Reader, was the total extent of my careers guidance!

I did determine some months later to take charge of a little of my destiny, and wrote a letter *on spec* addressed to the Works Manager at Eastleigh. I received a reply fairly quickly, inviting me for an interview and enclosing a ticket for my travel from Shanklin to Eastleigh on April 16 1958. I arrived at the works, and somewhat nervously was shown into the office of the Works Manager, Mr K H Morriss. His office, which was in the administration block, was large, and I remember that there were framed coats of arms of the Southern Railway and its constituent companies adorning the walls. I forget the precise nature of our conversation, but he seemed a kindly man to me, and he sketched out various employment possibilities, engineering, drawing office, and so on. [6]

In the course of his finding out a little about me we got on to the subject of education. "How's your maths?" he asked. That question again! At least this time I was able to answer that I had a GCE 'O' level in the subject, having at last managed to struggle through the hoop - just - during the previous winter. "I'm OK with arithmetic and geometry," I added, "but I have to admit algebra tends to elude me, because no-one has ever told me what it's used for." Mr Mor-

riss smiled, and gave me hope. He looked out of the window and said "Do you know, in all my time at work I don't think I have ever used algebra."

At the end of the interview it had been established that I had an unshakeable liking of the steam locomotive, and Mr Morriss had reminded me gently that the times were changing, and I was forced to agree. "Still," he said "You might as well see some steam locomotives and look at how we work on them while you are here." We stepped outside his office, where a young man in overalls was waiting, who he introduced to me as one of his star apprentices, before bidding me goodbye. This was obviously a pre-meditated kindness, because the apprentice was from my home town in the Isle of Wight. I suspect he was pleased to have a break from work, because he gave me a thorough and lengthy tour of the works and the adjacent motive power depot.

We visited every corner of the works. First we went to the foundry, and then to the pattern store, where there was an astounding quantity of interesting wooden artefacts used for creating the castings for parts for all manner of engines, probably including, so my new apprentice friend suggested, types which had been extinct for years.

On our way to the main body of the Works, my attention was drawn to a couple of ex-LNWR tenders, probably from Bowen-Cooke's 'Claughton' class 4-6-0s, still in LMS livery, and converted for oil-burning - a most unexpected find. I discovered later that they had probably arrived at Eastleigh in the mid 1940s, before the beginning of the Southern's short-lived venture into oil burning, and the reason for their presence was obscure. According to the guru R W Kidner [7] they were still there in 1965, although when I visited in the summer of that year they were nowhere to be seen.

Returning to my tour of the works, the erecting shop came next, followed by the boiler, wheel, tender and fitting shops. The erecting shop yielded the sight of a bent connecting rod removed from a Bulleid Pacific, visual evidence that the results of a severe slipping session were sometimes more than theatrical and noisy pyrotechnics. As might be expected the erecting shop contained much of interest, including nearly-overhauled Q 0-6-0 No. 30545 being fitted with a BR standard blast pipe and chimney, and USA No. 30064 stripped down to her bar frames. I was transported to another place when I saw on her smoke-box saddle the circular maker's plate reading 'Vulcan Ironworks – Wilkes-Barre –

6. My thanks to Alan Mew, author of the "eastleighworks.co.uk" website, and to Brian Foord, for confirming Mr Morriss's role.
7. Mentioned in his book "Service Stock of the Southern Railway", published by the Oakwood Press in 1993.

The curious affair of the LMS tenders. The top picture, probably by H C Casserley, taken on 22 September 1945, shows two LMS tenders at the dump at Eastleigh. The locomotive between them is ex-Isle of Wight A1X 0-6-0T W12, which languished at the dump from its departure from the Island in 1936 until April 1949. Interestingly, the tenders arrived before the Southern's excursion into oil burning. The lower picture, taken on my visit to Eastleigh on 16 April 1958, shows the tenders still in LMS livery (presumably they are the same ones) converted for use with oil burning locomotives.

Pennsylvania – 1943'. It was like a glimpse of another world an infinite distance away.

I was astounded at the din created by the pneumatic riveters used in the boiler shop, and maybe feared for my hearing a little. Impossible to contemplate in this day and age, there was not a set of ear defenders in sight, and, incidentally, nowhere in the whole works was there a hard hat. Moving outside the boiler shop, we had a look around the range of spare boilers held for various types of locomotives, including one for the H2 Brighton 'Atlantics'. At the time No. 32424 *Beachy Head* was the sole survivor of the class, soon to be withdrawn, and so the boiler was never to be required.

On from here the smith's shop, the research department and the forge were visited, together with the little paint shop which looked after nameplates, warning notices and the like.

Next on the menu was a visit to the motive power depot, via a quick detour past the device used for breaking up scrap for

recasting, which was effective, if unsophisticated. A wrecking ball, hoisted to the top of a tower, was let to drop on a pile of scrap. Health and safety was honoured here in some measure; the bottom of the tower was walled with old boiler plates to stop any sideways flying lumps of metal, and thus life and limb might have been safe.

Outstanding exhibit at the shed was the mighty ex-LSWR G16 4-8-0T No. 30495, newly out-shopped in unlined black freight livery, and doubtless awaiting running in. A number of other types of locomotive were, of course, in evidence, and there was a good representation of standard varieties. A sad sign of the changing times to which Mr Morriss had alluded was a long line of dead locomotives stored awaiting scrapping; included in it were ex-LBSC E2s and E4s, and ex-LSW T9s and M7s.

We wandered back to the works, where 0395 class 0-6-0 No. 30564 of 1881 was dawdling about on pilot duties. I

Top - *An immaculate 'G16' No. 30495, ex-works, and awaiting running-in. Seen at the rear of the running shed. 16 April 1958.*

Right - *On the same date, Nos, 34082 and 30859 are fresh from overhaul outside in the steaming shed outside the front of the works.*

noted how antiquated she looked with her sloped-back smoke box. In the manner of all pilots, she seemed to spend an inordinate amount of time doing very little. The tour concluded with a look at the steaming shed, where immaculate 'Lord Nelson' No. 30859, 'Battle of Britain' No. 34082 and Ivatt 2-6-2T 41302 were gently coming alive after overhaul. And steam locomotives *do* come alive when the fire is lit.

In those days we who had hopes that some way might be found to prolong the era of steam were surrounded by well-rehearsed arguments telling us why the steam locomotive was finished. It was thermally inefficient (ninety-seven or so percent of the heat generated by a conventional locomotive boiler was alleged to be exhausted unused through the chimney), it was only available for work for a limited period each day (diesels and electrics were available almost continuously, so we were told), and the daily maintenance of it was heavy and dirty. It also needed two men (and they were

men in those days) to operate it. Labour and fuel were becoming increasingly costly, too. On the other hand, the steam locomotive did have the advantages of relative simplicity as a machine, reasonably low first cost and, if it was a successful design, it could be long-lived.

I had been toying around with these apparent contradictions ever since I first learned a little about railway economics, and then in the spring of 1958 I had an idea. Why not, I thought, use electricity drawn from the third rail or overhead wire to create steam by way of immersion heaters in a boiler? And then, after using the steam to generate motion, return it to the boiler, perhaps after condensation, for a brief reheat? This closed-circuit system would require only limited back-up supplies of water, and no fuel, to be carried, thus saving weight and cost. All sorts of other devices would be used to enable the machine to function with efficiency and simplicity. I envisaged driving cabs at each end (*à la* "Leader") and direct drive turbines or divided drive

Had I been able to visit Eastleigh a few years earlier, I might have seen this sight on 26 August 1950. 'Atlantic' No. 2425 'Trevose Head' with 'Q' No. 30530, the latter by the coal stage alongside.

Denis Callender

reciprocating machinery with derived valve gear to create movement. And, moreover, it could be driven by one person. Overall, my logic, such as it was, and flawed as it might have been, was to use electricity generated very efficiently, perhaps by nuclear power, and convert it to traction at a distance by way of simple mechanical processes.

Because Mr Morriss at Eastleigh Works had already received me kindly, I was presumptuous enough to send him drawings of my proposed beast to for his comments, and was delighted to receive from him in return a further invitation to visit. So in June I was off to Eastleigh again, for a brief chat with him, after which he handed me on to his Chief Designer, a Mr Mills. Mr Mills talked with me about my ideas for upwards of an hour, and very gently let me understand that perhaps my proposals were not as perfect as I thought they were. I felt no sense of being put-down or patronised, and the discussion left me feeling really helped. I remember that he said with a wry smile, looking at my drawings "I'm not sure that some of the people here would really like another machine that looked like the 'Leader'. It was not too popular with several of those who worked with it!"

We talked about other things, too, which, of course, I much enjoyed, and he deliberated at some length on the American mechanical stokers that were to have been fitted to some ten 'Merchant Navies' in the early 1950's, and the Chief Mechanical Engineer Oliver Bulleid's deep disappointment that they weren't. I seem to remember that there was some inference that the National Coal Board was not interested in supplying coal of the right specification for the stokers, and Mr Mills said that he thought that their decision and the inevitable cancellation of the stoker scheme broke Bulleid's heart. Perhaps it might have done, but around the time of the cancellation Bulleid was becoming well ensconced in the Irish Republic, and was soon to be working hard on dieselising the CIE and making the experiments which assisted him in developing his last steam locomotive innovation, the turf burner CC1, son of the "Leader" as it were. It has been written that the 'Merchant Navy' boiler, even under test, never reached its absolute capacity for steam production because of the limitations of the human ability to stoke it. Maybe the proposed mechanical stokers could have enabled the boiler's maximum steam-raising capacity to have been realised, and this in turn might have made a difference to the life of the class, and possibly even the future of the steam locomotive in general. Somehow it seemed a little anticlimactic when, after my discussion with Mr Mills, I managed another visit to the erecting shop before I had to leave.

Alongside the coal stage at Eastleigh in May / June 1958. BR Standard types, Nos. 82016 and 76012, with in the distance an 'M7'.

Tony Molyneaux

I had something of an eyesight problem, which I had been warned might exclude me from some railway jobs, and after some parental consultation I wrote a letter to British Transport Commission Headquarters asking for their views. Back came a reply summoning me to Marylebone Station, where the BTC was resident in those days. When I got there I was ushered into what seemed to me to be a palatial office occupied by a gentleman whose name I forget, who spoke with me about various possibilities. I recall that he had a very large desk, the top of which was inlaid with green leather decorated with gold around the edge. The desk was one of those grand ancient specimens, known, I believe, as a "Partner's Desk", which not only had drawers on the business side, as it were, but on the front of the pillars also. The drawers, naturally, boasted brass handles.

After talking for a while, the gentleman behind the desk organised a thorough eye-test for me. Where it took place, I'm not sure, but it was truly thorough. At its end, I was told that my sight restrictions meant that I could not be employed in any work connected with the operation of trains, which rather limited the range of jobs that might be available to me. This was not an entirely unexpected piece of news, but the affirmation that many possibilities were beyond my reach was received with a heavy heart. As some-

thing of a sop, I was told to report to a manager in the Southern Region's administrative headquarters at Waterloo on my way home to get some sort of idea about the kind of vacancies for which I might be eligible.

Although obviously busy, the manager gave me something of a run-down on some potential options, mainly clerical, but few had much attraction. Towards the end of our talk he remarked that there was at that time a vacancy in the part of the organisation that dealt with posters, and that I could have a chat with the section head if I wished. This sounded a little more interesting than some of the pen-pushing things that had been described so far, and I went along with the suggestion. If I had any notions that the job in question was likely to be involved with creative things the energetic shirt-sleeved section head quickly dispelled them. It was simply a junior post whose chief responsibility was sending out bundles of posters to be pasted on the hoardings at stations. I asked how much the salary was. The section head grinned wryly. "You'll never get rich working on the railway," he replied, and went on to mention a sum which I think was a fraction less than four pounds a week. "You could start next week, if you wanted," he went on. I declined the offer, I hope courteously, and boarded the train home to lick my wounds.

There was a final twist to my search for a railway-related job. Besides my long-standing passion for the railway, I was also very interested in film and the cinema, and it crossed my mind that there was a body called British Transport Films, and so I contacted them. I was asked to visit their office in London, and had a friendly interview with the organisation's head, the late Edgar Anstey. In my naivety at time, I was unaware that I was in the presence of someone pretty famous who was a distinguished figure in the British Documentary movement. A little later than my meeting with him he was responsible for launching the late John Schlesinger's career as a director by asking him to direct the award-winning film 'Terminus', about a day in the life of Waterloo station, released in 1961. Schlesinger, of course, went on to become a great power in the land of the cinema, his most famous offering probably being 'Midnight Cow-boy'. Sadly, Edgar Anstey perceived no latent cinematographic talent of any usable sort in me, and my final effort to work with railways withered on the vine.

My outstanding memory of all the gentlemen from Eastleigh, Marylebone, Waterloo and British Transport Films was that they gave me of their time and experience generously, even if it transpired that I was to be of little use to them. The words 'courtesy' and 'kindness' spring to mind.

My fairly brief skirmish with the possibilities of a railway career was over. From here on, with some regrets, I reverted to my former role of devoted observer and aficionado.

A wet 25 June 1958, at Eastleigh. No. 35022 'Holland America Line' hurtles through with the down Bournemouth Belle.

5

Aside from the journeys involved with my searches for employment, I made a good number of forays from the Isle of Wight to the mainland in 1958 and 1959.

In April 1958 I fetched up again at good old reliable Fareham. On the way I noted a surprising lack of steam at Portsmouth and Southsea, brought about by the recent appearance of the new two-car Hampshire diesel units. Revealing my bias, my notes record them as noisy and uncomfortable to ride in at slow speeds, and smelling of diesel fuel (which, all things considered, was perhaps not surprising!). Steam was still around on shed at Fratton, with two N15s and a U. I paused a while at Cosham, where two further N15s and another U went about their business, and sometime later caught another of my new-found diesel friends to Fareham. At Fareham 700 class 0-6-0 No. 30316 was station pilot, and after a while wandered off in the direction of Gosport with a solitary general utility van in tow. There is something here about the economics of railway operation in those days:

even if the van had been loaded with gold bars (which clearly it wasn't), the cost of running the locomotive, the two enginemen and the guard would clearly not have been covered, and this was only one such occurrence on one day. Imagine that extended nationwide. The financial fate of the railway was becoming obvious, even to me. Hopefully slightly more profitable were the other trains observed, which included two expresses, one Cardiff bound, and the other heading for Plymouth, both hauled by Bulleid Light Pacifics.

My next mainland visit involved a trip to Bognor Regis, which was largely Southern Electric focused. Various types of two and four car units were around, including one or two specimens of the by then rather ancient looking 2-NOL type in their last year of service. Amongst minor observations, I noted the division of twelve-coach trains from Victoria at Barnham Junction. The first unit went on to Portsmouth, and the remaining two took the branch to Bognor. Thinking

On the same day, recently rebuilt No. 35002 'Union Castle' waits on the down platform line, with a running-in turn to Southampton, whilst 'T9' No. 30707 trundles north, possibly destined for the east yard, with a mixed freight.

Above - 2-BIL set No. 2079 at Bognor Regis. 17 April 1958.

Opposite top - The products of Mr Drummond still in use after almost six decades. '700' No. 30697 and 'M7' No. 30132 at Guildford on 18 may 1961. My next sighting of the former was on the scrap line at Exeter St Davids in September 1963.

Opposite bottom - Guildford shed looking south on 18 May 1961, showing the rather restricted space that it occupied. Left to right are shed pilot, 'B4' No. 30089, 'Q1' 33005 and 'N' 31414.

back, the Southern seemed to divide and join together trains more than the other railways and regions. I suppose that the record for the number destinations served by portions of a train must have been held by the late lamented "Atlantic Coast Express", the main summer Saturday service of which in the 1950's and early 1960's was divided at Exeter into two parts. The first went on to Plymouth, leaving portions for Bude and Padstow at Okehampton, which in turn were split at Halwill Junction. The second part travelled on to Barnstaple Junction, where it was separated into portions, one for Torrington and one for Ilfracombe.

On another day I visited Portsmouth to make a fruitless search for remains of the Fratton and East Southsea branch, closed in 1914 and lifted in 1926, whose route was clearly marked by the road layout shown on the Ordnance Survey map. I discovered nothing whatever, but thought that I did detect conspicuous gaps in rows of houses and non-matching brickwork in some garden walls which seemed to point to the route. As some recompense, there was an interesting service electric unit in the sidings at Fratton, obviously, I thought, converted from steam-hauled coaches, and probably in turn converted again from early revenue-earning

electric stock. Maybe it was part of an old 3-SUB unit. The coaches were individually numbered DS349 and DS350, and the set as a whole was numbered 91.

Through the year there were a few journeys to London. Various types of British Railways locomotives passed in and out of my gaze, but there was other motive power which provided additional interest, and which was more often than not in its appropriate position at various points on the way to the metropolis.

The first was at the extensive Hilsea Gasworks which, as with all such plants in those days, used huge quantities of coal. This required a comprehensive internal rail system, and the works had its own pair of steam locomotives. These were Beyer Peacock 0-4-0ST's and were both named. No. 1 was *Sir John Baker*. Sir John (1829-1909), a noted local dignitary, was sometime Liberal MP for Portsmouth and was twice elected Mayor of the Borough (Portsmouth didn't become a City until 1926). Apparently he was known as "Honest John": I can't help wondering how he would have got on in politics today. With his reputation and his parliamentary and civic service he was, therefore, very worthy of having a locomotive named for him. No. 2 was more prosaically named *Farlington* after an adjacent district of Portsmouth. Both engines were always kept immaculate, at least when I saw them, and one of them always seemed to be in evidence as I passed the gasworks by on the main line.

The next interesting machine was further to the north and observed always from a 4-COR tearing past, was on the Longmoor Military Railway, which had its southern extremity at Liss. Idly, I sometimes wondered how many square miles of northern Hampshire were given over to military activity. The LMR was frustrating because its presence was only known by a fleeting glimpse as the fast train to London hurtled by, and it had an air of mystery about it. Nearly every time I was whisked past, a brightly blue painted diesel shunter, the fixture in question and I think four-wheeled, was there, sporting 'LMR 829' in large white letters and numerals.

The third interesting appliance was much closer to Waterloo. At this time Durnsford Road Power Station – between Wimbledon and Earlsfield – was still generating electricity for the Southern system, although soon to be closed. Again, it was a place which consumed much coal, and for years shared a Bo-Bo electric shunting locomotive with the Wimbledon electric train depot. It was an odd-looking affair. Like most from its era it had what could technically be called a steeple cab. As I recall, however, the body seemed more like a metal garden shed with protuberances at each end. All the books said that it was numbered 74S, but it was always so dirty whenever I saw it that I was never able to distinguish the number for myself. The power station closed in 1958, but I believe the locomotive lingered into the mid-1960's.

Late 1958 also yielded another trip to Stratford-on-Avon, this time for 'Much Ado About Nothing', although the

Left - Ex-pat turned native. Bulleid 1Co-Co1 diesel-electric No. 10203 on shed at Willesden. 14 May 1959.

Bottom - Continental Victoria, 6 June 1960. A small crowd awaits the arrival of passengers from the 'Golden Arrow' which has just arrived. The light pacific which has just brought the train in is just visible on the right.

'S15' No. 30824 brings a Feltham bound freight through Staines on a hot 18 June 1960.

play's title certainly didn't apply to the pleasure of journeying a third of the way up England and back in a day by a steam-hauled train. The railway routine was much as in the previous year, but none the less enjoyable for all that. Again we changed engines at Basingstoke, and our S15 produced a particularly spirited performance on the return run, taking the lion's share of the credit for reducing a forty minute deficit caused by a Western engine failure somewhere north of Moreton-in-the-Marsh to a mere quarter of an hour late arrival at Portsmouth Harbour.

1959 marked my last year as an Isle of Wight resident, and there were quite a few trips to the mainland. London, sometimes as a staging post to somewhere else, was the principal destination. A variety of steam locomotives were still extant, but I noted that the M7s were gradually being eclipsed as station pilots at Waterloo by various types including

E4 0-6-2Ts and invading ex-GWR 5700 0-6-0 panniers. I also acquired a nodding acquaintance with the Waterloo and City tube, still then the property of the Southern Region, and remember that the 1940 stock still looked good. Another Southern Electric observation, at Waterloo East, was of the two Bulleid four-car double-deck units coupled together and filled to the brim with rush hour travellers.

Probably one of the best railway days of the year was what was to become my final visit to the Hayling Island branch in April. I think that the day started reasonably sunny, and certainly the sun shone at Hayling Island as the engine of the day – my old friend No. 32646 once more – deposited me there. As I wandered around she came and went on other workings, and later took on a little fuel at the coal stage, still in the sunshine. I remember, though, that when we arrived back at Havant it was pouring heavily with rain.

Above and opposite. *Hayling Island and Havant, 9 April 1959. The branch locomotive, on this day No. 32646, was based at Fratton, and spent all day shuttling to and fro on the branch, with replenishment of the coal from time to time a necessity. Coal was available at Hayling Island, and all topping up was done by hand. At the top, opposite, are the LBSCR starting signals at Hayling Island. The middle picture shows No. 32646 departing with a train for Havant as the weather closes in. the lower picture shows the little train left isolated and somewhat forlorn alongside the puddle strewn platform after arrival at Havant, with a carriage door left open by the rapidly departing passengers.*

When the station was rebuilt in 1938, the Southern Railway had not seen fit to equip the bay platform serving the Hayling Island branch with an awning, and so there was a stampede of passengers for shelter, and the little train was left looking isolated and somewhat forlorn alongside the puddle strewn platform, with a carriage door left open by the departing travellers. Rain notwithstanding, it was once more a pleasing little excursion, enhanced, with my constantly growing knowledge of railway apparatus, by the discovery that Hayling Island's two starting signals were still splendid wooden LB&SCR lower quadrants.

A summer trip to London – the school Railway Club again – and a visit to the Midland Region's Willesden Motive Power Depot introduced me to the Southern's Bulleid 1Co-Co1 diesel electric design. No.10203, now comfortably working on the LNW main line, well away from its roots,

was discovered on shed looking quite at home, obviously well cared for by its custodians, and beautifully cleaned and polished.

By now this chapter of my Southern residence was on the wane, and in the autumn of 1959 I left my much-loved Isle of Wight for work in the Thames Valley and later in East Anglia. During this enforced exile there were long Southern-less periods, particularly during my residence in Suffolk. The Thames Valley kept me vaguely in touch with Southern stuff, providing visits to London termini, Windsor and Eton Riverside, with its fine William Tite designed buildings, and the more mundane stations at Staines and Twickenham. I rediscovered Richmond station, which still had signs for the Southern Railway, the LMS and London Transport advertising its presence to the outside world. There was also always the possibility of seeing some Southern activity at Reading, including through trains to and from the Western Region.

The visits to London termini had a few high spots. At Victoria the neon-lit "Golden Arrow" sign over the entrance to the platform where the train arrived with passengers from Paris clearly indicated that it was still an example of rail sophistication that mattered, even though as an example of international prestige its days were numbered. On a totally different tack, when I arrived on one trip to Waterloo there was little of the customary bustle, and things were more or less at a standstill. This was because a train arriving from Portsmouth had had a small altercation with the coaches of a Weymouth-bound express, and both had blocked a number of the lines into the station. I think all was cleared in less than a couple of hours. Today, things would probably have closed down for the day, at least!

I made trips back to the Isle of Wight in the spring of 1960 and the early summer of 1961, on the latter entering Southern territory again at Reading South. Today the presence of this three platform terminus, together with locomotive shed, seems impossible to envisage. All traces of the railway have long gone, and the site is completely redeveloped. On the occasion of my journey I noted brisk traffic on the run to Guildford, where I was to board a Portsmouth-bound electric. At Guildford I found a pleasing lack of diesel power, only a single shunter being present. There was, also pleasingly, a variety of steam types in evidence, including representatives of classes Q1, M7, N and 700, and, most pleasingly of all, one of the last remaining ex-LSW B4 0-4-0Ts, number No. 30089, working out the twilight of its days in the role of shed pilot, engaged in removing clinker from the ash pits in a standard 16-ton mineral wagon. During my wait for the train to Portsmouth interest was aroused by a working from Horsham headed by an Ivatt Class 2 2-6-2T towing two Maunsell corridor coaches converted to a push-pull set, with an ex-SEC ten compartment non-corridor coach, match-boarded below the waist and carrying the number S1092S, tacked on behind.

Towards the end of 1961 I migrated to East Anglia, where complete modernisation had happened, and for the next two years I almost forgot what a steam locomotive looked like. This state of affairs was rectified in the late summer of 1963, when I spent some leisure days in Devon. The break turned out to be a precursor to a permanent move to the county, and to re-establishing my fond and much-missed link with things Southern.

Incident at Waterloo: Friday 3 June 1960

"6.32 p.m., Friday, 3rd June 1960.

The 6,14 p.m. Down steam passenger train from Waterloo to Weymouth (unidentified 'Merchant navy' and 11 coaches) which was well filled with Whitsun holiday traffic, left from No. 12 platform at 6,31 p,m,, on a fine evening, with the route set to the Down Main Through line (delay in departure caused by heavy traffic). It had travelled only some 280 yards when the 6.12 p.m, Up electric empty coaching stock train from Durnsford Road to Waterloo (12 cars - 4COR unit No. 3119 leading), on the Up Main Through line, came into facing sidelong collision with it. The latter train was destined for No, 6 platform; its route crossed that of the steam train and it was therefore to have been stopped at the inner home signal, but it passed

that signal at danger. The trains struck each other offside to offside at a point 92 yards beyond the signal and near the converging junction on the paths of the two trains.

The leading motor coach of the electric train struck the fourth coach of the steam train and the electric train stopped immediately with the front half of the leading coach ripped away. The steam train however continued on its journey and the sides of all the coaches rearwards from the point of impact were damaged; many window lights were broken and doors and side panels were torn off or buckled. Neither train was derailed. There were 671 passengers in the steam train but fortunately, apart from a few cases of slight cuts or shock, there were no injuries. The motorman of the electric train also was uninjured. The steam train was stopped at Vauxhall the next station (the Guard of the steam train was travelling in the ninth coach and states he felt the impact. After this vehicle had passed the point of impact he looked out but seeing no derailment allowed the train to continue to Vauxhall where he stopped the train by means of his brake valve, this also allowed for ease is emptying the service). Passengers were returned to Waterloo in suburban trains and continued their journeys by subsequent main line trains.

The Assistant Station Master, Waterloo, was in the signal box at the time and saw the collision, he promptly called for the ambulance and fire services. These arrived within a few minutes but their help was not required. Fallen metal from one of the trains caused a dead short circuit between the conductor rail and the running rail which automatically cut off the traction current to the lines concerned.

The electric train was removed (initially brought forward into the station as seen above) and the Up and Down Main Through lines were re-opened to traffic at 8.15 p.m. after they had been examined and tests had been carried out, but these and other lines were re-closed subsequently for various periods to enable further tests to be made on the signalling equipment. Very considerable delays were caused to the train service generally with Up trains waiting to enter Waterloo held at every signal as far out as Wimbledon.

The driver of the empty electric train was adamant he had received a green signal to run into No. 6 platform, he maintained this view throughout. This green aspect was also initially confirmed by the Guard of the same set. The driver of the departing steam train was similarly adamant he had received the correct indication to leave the station, confirmed by the guard of that train, station staff and men in Waterloo signal box. As the accident happened, one of the two signalmen on duty had shouted to the Assistant Station Master that a run-past had taken place.

In view of the dispute over the evidence and the suggestion there may have been a defect in the signalling, the Inspecting Officer Col. McMullen assisted by Col. Reed carried out considerable testing but no defect was found. The driver of the empty electric unit was therefore considered to have been responsible."

(Taken from the official report on the collision published on 30 September 1960.)

Opposite page, top - *Interested onlookers gaze towards the throat of the station and the damaged electric train.*

Opposite page, bottom - *N15 No. 30450 'Sir Kay' and M7 No. 30035 marooned in the station until track is cleared.*

This page - *Damaged 4-COR electric unit No. 3119 eventually enters the station very gingerly.*

Reading General (Western Region), May 1960. 'C' class 0-6-0 No. 31722 from Guildford trundles through from the direction of Scours Lane with a mixed freight no doubt bound for its home metals.

No. 41307, the Exeter Central station pilot, 6 September 1963, seen in the process of detaching a van from a parcels train. 6 September 1963

6

I look back happily to the pleasure I felt in encountering steam and Southern things again. I had never visited the West Country as an adult, so there was the added delight of discovering the cities and towns, the coastal resorts, the verdant countryside and the wilds of the moors. And, of course, there were the fabled railway locations such as Honiton Bank and Exmouth Junction and The Withered Arm, otherwise known as the Southern main line between Okehampton and Padstow, which became realities, even if some were on their last legs.

For the break in early September 1963 I was actually based off Southern territory at Torquay, and a little time was spent visiting the ex-GW Exe Valley to Tiverton and the Culm Valley branch to Hemyock, both of which were about to be executed, at least as far as passengers were concerned. It goes without saying, though, that it was the Southern which claimed most of my attention, and my first priority was to travel to Exeter Central, where plenty of steam activity awaited me, much of it, satisfyingly, involving Southern types, although there was a substantial representation of Ivatt Class 2 2-6-2Ts and BR Standard varieties.

I lingered awhile and watched Class 2-6-2T No. 41307 fiddling around on pilot duties, and enjoyed the sight of N class 2-6-0 31840 heading east with a splendidly mixed freight train. It seems almost impossible now to conceive of the variety of wagons and merchandise carried by the average general goods trains of those days, and in a curious kind of way I can't help wondering whether individual motor vehicles thrashing up and down motorways emitting noxious effluvia and clogging up towns and villages has advanced the cause of commerce as much as some might think.

When a little time had elapsed, there came the sound of locomotives working hard, a sound which reached a crescendo as W class 2-6-4T No. 31915 and Standard class 4 2-6-4T No. 80035 breasted the 1 in 37 incline from Exeter St Davids double-heading a heavy ballast train from Meldon Quarry. And two locomotives at the head was not all. The train was banked in the rear by two more members of the W class, Nos. 31924 and 31914.

After delighting in the busy-ness of Exeter Central, I continued with my travels for the day, and took a train down the

Exeter Central with No. 31840 heading east with a mixed train. 6 September 1963.

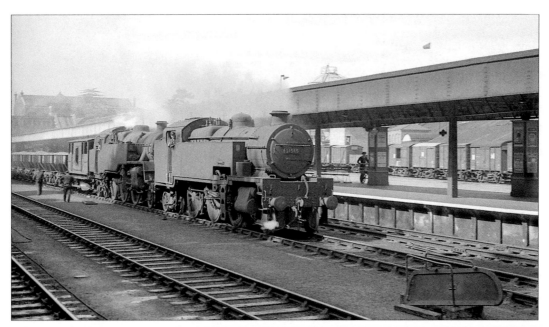

Exeter Central, 6 September 1963, with the ballast train from Meldon referred to on the previous page. At the head is 'W' No. 31915, leading BR Class 4 2-6-4T No. 80035. Pushing hard at the rear of the train behind the ballast plough brake-van are two more members of the 'W' class, Nos. 31924 and 31914. This would be the last month any member of the class was active from Exmouth Junction. At the start of the year eight had been shown as 'on the books' at the depot although this had dwindled to five by September.

Exmouth branch. At this time Western Region DMUs were gradually infiltrating, but steam was still around, and Standard Class 2 2-6-2T No. 82001 was helping out with services.

I spent a spell absorbing the scene at Exmouth and then took a train to Tipton St Johns, the somewhat unlikely and sometimes busy junction where the line from Exmouth met the tracks of the branch from Sidmouth Junction to Sidmouth. My train was headed by No. 41322, and we passed an Exmouth bound train drawn by No. 41318 at Budleigh Salterton. This town, much beloved of retired officers from the services and commuters to Exeter, most of them rather upmarket, once enjoyed a fast rush-hour service to Exeter Central, by means of a reversal at Exmouth, at a civilised commuting time in the morning, with a return working at a similarly civilised hour in the afternoon.

My train terminated at Tipton St Johns, where No. 41322 ran around and prepared for the return to Exmouth, whilst I boarded a train drawn by sister engine No. 41320 for the short run to Sidmouth, which started with quite a sharp grade. I paused at Sidmouth to look around. The station seemed surrounded by genteel greenery and although the building displayed a 'British railways' sign, Southern influence was still very much present, and, indeed all was probably much as it had been for several decades. The place was still busy, and there was still apparently good freight traffic, as well as plenty of passengers. With all the branch lines travelled that day there was an increasing rumble of possible closure, but in my mind what I had seen in terms of usage gave a lie to the possibility. The train service wasn't bad, either, and the day I went wasn't even a Saturday when maximum business might have been expected.

East Devon branches, 6 September 1963.

1 - 41322 and 41318 pass at Budleigh Salterton.
2 - 82001 and a WR DMU at Exmouth
3 - Tipton St Johns, with the line to Sidmouth heading off up the incline to the left.
4 - 41320 at Sidmouth after having brought in a train from Sidmouth Junction,.

Sidmouth station, 6 September 1963. Still very much Southern Railway place, and busy after the arrival of the afternoon train.

In due course I made the trip from Sidmouth to Sidmouth Junction. It had turned into a glorious late summer's day, and as I arrived at Sidmouth Junction on the branch train my heart was gladdened by the sight of 'Merchant Navy' no. 35006 *Peninsular & Oriental S.N. Co.* spanking in on the main line with a Waterloo bound express. As she paused, her safety valve lifted in readiness for the sunlit climb towards Honiton and the distant hills, slightly misty with a heat haze, before she made a marvellously exhibitionist departure. For the rest of my stay there was a fine procession of trains in each direction, all steam operated, and I returned to Exeter by way of the main line well pleased with my first exploration of East Devon.

The following day, on the way to witness the death throes of the Exe and Culm Valley lines, I stopped for a time at Exeter St Davids, where I happily observed the Southern comings and goings on this, the last Saturday of the summer timetable for that year. These included the Surbiton to Okehampton car carrier, headed by 'West Country' 4-6-2 34096 *Trevone*. Two of the W class 2-6-4T's, Nos. 31914 and

31924 again, were standing by to assist trains up to Exeter Central, today in the company of 5700 class pannier tank No. 4692. I was also able to wander around the declining motive power depot where there was the by then fairly usual line of dead locomotives, the majority inevitably destined for scrapping, alongside which I ambled rather sadly. Amongst others in this disconsolate row there were three 700 class 0-6-0s, Nos. 30687, 30697 and 30700, the first of which had been withdrawn from service three years before, and a lone M7 0-4-4T, No. 30125. I couldn't help feeling a little more sadness about the third Southern type in the scrap line, I suppose because it brought back memories from more than a dozen years previously of a sunny day at Hythe in Hampshire. It was, of course, the Z class, to which I bade a final farewell through the silent and derelict No. 30951, lately withdrawn from banking duties between Exeter St Davids and Exeter Central.

After this expedition I returned to a steam-less East Anglia for a while, and then moved permanently to the West Country in February 1964. For the journey from London I opted

Left - Sidmouth Junction, 6 September 1963 with No. 35006 'Peninsular & Oriental S.N. Co.' heading a Waterloo bound express. As she paused her safety valve lifted in readiness for the sunlit climb towards Honiton and the distant hills. The departure was marvellously exhibitionist.

Right, top - Exeter St Davids Middle signal box and its notorious level crossing, with No. 31849 piloting No. 34066 'Spitfire' and with the bankers, fronted by No. 31924 waiting alongside. 7 September 1963.

Right, bottom - The Surbiton to Okehampton car–carrier leaving Exeter St Davids on the last leg of its journey with No. 34096 'Trevone' in charge passing bankers 31914 and 4692. 7 September 1963.

Out to grass at Exeter St Davids shed, 7 September 1963. 'M7', No 30125, had been derelict for some months having been withdrawn at the end of 1962. In the right background there is another line of locomotives, including 700's and a member of the 'Z' class, also awaiting scrapping.

No. 34052 'Lord Dowding' with ballast from Meldon approaching Sidmouth Junction. 6 September 1963.

to travel from Waterloo and was pleased to find that there was still steam to be seen on trains heading in the direction of Bournemouth and Weymouth and on the road to points further west. The run was a little slower than the route from Paddington could offer although the fare was identical, but I enjoyed the ride behind a 'Merchant Navy' into the deepening winter twilight, and there were some stirringly fast stretches accompanied by the exhilarating sound of steam at speed.

As summer became a reality in 1964, it was clear that the old order on the Southern in the West Country was not going to last much longer. The East Devon branches were gradually being penetrated by Western Region diesel multiple units, and they had assumed virtually complete control by the end of the year. As the summer progressed 'Warship' and 'Hymek' diesel-hydraulics were appearing on the Waterloo main line. There was, therefore, something of a need to scurry to visit places and to record the final throes of the disappearing *status quo*.

That summer there were many trips to Exeter from the Western-served resort where I now lived. I also travelled to Portsmouth Harbour by way of Salisbury for a valedictory

trip to the Isle of Wight system, visited Seaton Junction and the Seaton branch a couple of times, and later made excursions to the rest of the East Devon system, as well as heading west on a few occasions.

The Seaton branch was already dieselised, but an advantage of this was the forward vision through the driver's cab offered by the railcar, and it was a pleasant ride through the countryside to meet the bird-watchers delight of the Axe estuary for the final part of the journey. I particularly remember the fine Victorian cast-iron urinal, which survives today, on the platform at Colyford, and it was pleasing to find that Seaton Station, Western railcar or not, still felt very Southern. Seaton Junction with its two through roads between the stopping lines was a great place to watch trains. Non-stopping workings in the up direction came hammering down off Honiton Bank, and those in the down direction were gathering speed in readiness for the climb. I particularly remember the Okehampton to Surbiton Car Carrier galloping through with 'West Country' No. 34092 *City of Wells* piloting Standard Class 5 No. 73082, carrying the assumed 'King Arthur' name of *Camelot*.

The next outing saw me spend an afternoon at Yeoford, the

No. 34092' 'City of Wells' and Standard No. 73082 'Camelot' approaching Seaton Junction at speed with the Okehampton - Surbiton car-carrier. 13 June 1964.

station nearest the junction of the Barnstaple and Okehampton lines. The new order was well in evidence here, and I saw only two trains, one of which was the car carrier and the other a milk working, hauled by steam.

I successfully sought permission from the authorities to visit Exmouth Junction, then the largest steam shed left in the West Country, and my July visit there, which lasted around three hours, yielded but three ex-Southern types – 'Merchant Navy' and unrebuilt 'West Country' Pacifics, and N class 2-6-0s. Others noted were a Standard Class 5 4-6-0, Standard Class 4 2-6-4Ts and a Class 2 2-6-2T, together with 5700 class 0-6-0PTs and the ubiquitous Ivatt Class 2 2-6-2Ts. The Southern was clearly in decline.

I revisited Sidmouth Junction to find diesels almost completely in control on the branches to Sidmouth and Exmouth. Although services had been reduced a little from former times, traffic, both freight and passenger, still seemed good, and there seemed no perceptible sniff of death in the air. Whatever the economics, the railways hereabouts still ran through idyllic English countryside. Three successive stations on the way from Sidmouth Junction to Exmouth – Ottery St Mary, Tipton St Johns and Newton Poppleford – had music in their names. Even better, Newton Poppleford served the community of Colaton Raleigh, where the Elizabethan Sir Walter, of cloak over the puddle and tobacco fame, was baptised. I had a passing thought that the resonance of the names carried with it something of the essence of all our images of Merrie England. Somehow the branch lines fitted with that, particularly on sunny days.

At the beginning of August I rode the train to Honiton and walked two miles or so, mainly uphill, to a bridge where a lane crossed the railway not far from the eastern portal of the tunnel which marked the summit of Honiton Bank, there to photograph the summer Saturday traffic. During the four hours or thereabouts that I was there, I found it heartening that there was only one diesel working, and that was a 'Warship' grinding up the gradient with the 11-30am Brighton to Plymouth express. All the rest of the ascending and descending trains were in the hands of 'Merchant Navy' and Light Pacifics (both original and rebuilt varieties) – and Standard Class 4 4-6-0s.

During the same month I twice visited Broad Clyst, a wayside station halfway between Exeter Central and Sidmouth Junction. As well as being a good place to photograph trains, it was also home to a Permanent Way Department Depot which had its own locomotive, a small Ruston and Hornsby four-wheeled diesel, No. DS1169, built for the Bristol Aviation Co in 1946, and purchased from them by

One of only two steam-hauled trains seen during a visit to Yeoford on sunny 20 June 1964. This is Class 3 No. 82044 heading a milk train.

Still very Southern, in spite of the presence of railcar W55016, this is Seaton station, inside and out, on 13 June 1964.

Exeter Central - Summer 1964.

Left - *Three 'Pacifics', almost straining at the leash to take up duty. From front to rear they are No. 34033 'Chard', 34066 'Spitfire' and 34015 'Exmouth'. 13 June 1964.*

Bottom - *No. 34080 '74 Squadron' waiting to reverse to Exmouth Junction for servicing. 4 July 1964*

Opposite top - *Class 5 No. 73161 with a local working from Seaton Junction. 27 June 1964.*

Opposite bottom - *The aftermath of steam, and a different use for a water crane: station staff, under the watchful eye of authority, put out a fire on the track where a locomotive has been standing. 27 June 64.*

Exmouth Junction Shed, 17 June 1964.

Top - *L to R, Nos. 80038, 31853, 34002 ' Salisbury', 31859 and 41295.*
Bottom - *The Grafton 2-ton steam crane. This was used for lifting buckets of clinker and ask when clearing the disposal roads. .*
Opposite top - *No. 34002 'Salisbury' being turned. 17 July 1964.*
Bottom right - *No. 41295 being coaled alongside an unidentified member of the 'N' class. .*

Honiton Bank - 1 August 1964.

Main view - No. 34057 'Biggin Hill' on the 11.15 Waterloo-Bude-Padstow express.

Top right - No. 73044 descending the gradient on the 11.00 Plymouth - Brighton.

Bottom right - No. 35016 'Elder Fyffes' with the 11.45 Waterloo to Ilfracombe express.

Left - Conversation piece at Exeter Central, 8 August 1964. The crew of No. 34030 'Watersmeet' on the 15.35 Exeter Central - Yeovil junction chat with another driver going off duty.

Above - Broad Clyst permanent way depot with the resident shunter, DS1169. 8 August 1964.

Right - LSWR platform furniture, still in fine condition, at Broad Clyst in August 1964.

British Railways in 1948. After seeing service at Folkestone Warren, it was transferred to Broad Clyst around 1960. It was a pretty unremarkable machine, but it was something different from the run-of-the-mill stuff normally found operating around such installations and that gave it a little charm. There was still a large quantity of pre-grouping items around at this time, and a particularly fine array of LSWR oil lamps sprouted from the platforms at Broad Clyst.

At this memoir enters its final passages I am conscious of a few wheels in my life turning a full circle. I have already mentioned my last trip to the Isle of Wight, which could be said to be the first wheel. The second related to time before the family's few months stay in Somerset in 1944 when we had lived for a time at Callington in East Cornwall. I recall little about this chapter of my life, and certainly nothing of the railway there. This may well be because, although Callington had a station, it was a long way from the town – the best part of a mile up the Launceston Road close to the hamlet of Kelly Bray – and I don't think that we ever used the train there. This particular wheel turning towards its full circle was signified by a trip I made on the Bere Alston to Callington branch in the summer of 1964. Steam still hung

on. That day there were some trains on the main line hauled by steam, but the Callington branch was still wholly the preserve of Ivatt Class 2 2-6-2Ts, usually towing a couple of Maunsell corridor coaches. It was an interesting run from Bere Alston. There was the massive viaduct over the Tamar at Calstock, which gave an aerial view of the slightly down-at-heel quay through which the products transported by the 3' 6" gauge East Cornwall Mineral Railway, predecessor to the standard gauge branch, were shipped. Almost everywhere throughout the route were signs of the former heavy industrial nature of the area, and as the line climbed from Calstock towards Callington through increasingly slightly bleak country to run round the foot of Kit Hill, there were relics a-plenty in the form of disused and crumbling mine engine houses and overgrown quarries and spoil heaps.

This page, modernisation in east Devon, 25 July 1964. **Top** *- Tipton St Johns, Swindon 3-car diesel unit headed by W51577 making up the 16.05 Sidmouth Junction - Exmouth, passes W51313 on the 16.18 to Sidmouth.*
Bottom *- The terminus at Sidmouth, BRCW 3-car diesel unit, headed by W51313 forming the 16.05 to Tipton St Johns. Upon arrival at the latter station the unit will reverse ready to return to Sidmouth.*

No. 34020 'Seaton' departing Broad Clyst with the 16.42 all stations, Exeter Central to Salisbury, 22 August 1964. On the left is a train of Invalid Carriages (as they used to be called) ready for despatch. The manufacturers of these was based not far away.

Scenes at Bere Alston and Calstock, 15 August 1964.

Opposite top - *Nos. 41307 after arrival with the 16.25 train from Callington.*

Opposite bottom - *From the vantage point of the footbridge, No. 41206 heading the 13.00 (SO) train to Callington.*

Above - *Sister engine, No. 41317 at the down main platform with the 12.52 short Tavistock to Plymouth working.*

Bottom - *The towering viaduct at Calstock viewed from train from Callington. The glass houses in the foreground serve to remind us of the fruit traffic which was once so important to the line.*

Callington and Calstock , 15 August 1964.

Opposite top - No. 41206 preparing to couple to the coaches prior to stabling them.

Opposite centre - The same engine assembling a train of vans.

Opposite bottom - No. 41307 awaiting departure with the 16.25 to Bere Alston.

Above - Cleaning the smokebox of No. 41206, whilst water is being taken prior to the locomotive being put away for the weekend.

Right - Curious visitor to Calstock. My feeling is that this slightly ancient wagon, D1396, is actually from the fleet of Admiralty Devenport Dockyard vehicles. The question is, if so what was it doing at Calstock?

There still seemed to be lively traffic at Callington. After the arrival of our train, our locomotive – No. 41206 – indulged in a little gentle shunting in the yard, putting together a train which consisted mainly of empty vans. She then removed the coaches from the platform and parked them on the stock siding parallel to the platform road, and attended the engine shed road, where she had her smokebox cleaned out by the fireman whilst her motion was oiled by the driver, before retiring to the shed for the weekend. The vans were probably evidence that fertilizer into and fruit traffic from the fertile Tamar Valley was still very much in existence, although not for much longer. A couple of years after my visit the line was closed for freight, and shut down completely between Gunnislake and Callington. Fortunately, the Gunnislake-Bere Alston-Plymouth sections remain as a 'basic railway' and retain a passenger service to this day. Thus, thankfully, amongst other things, the towering viaduct at Calstock survives.

In early September I travelled east to Axminster. It was the final Saturday of the summer timetable, and, I think, the final day when the 'Atlantic Coast Express' and some other workings were hauled by steam. That day the "ACE" was in two sections, the first drawn by a Light Pacific and the second by a .Merchant Navy'. After watching the procession of both up and down expresses, I took a train on the Lyme Regis branch which had less than three months to live

before complete closure. It is an everlasting sadness to me that I was a little too late to be taken down the line by one of the graceful Adams' Radial 4-4-2Ts. Instead, the ride was in one of the by now nearly omnipresent Western Region diesel units, this time three single unit cars working in multiple. The forward vision through the cab again provided good views of the railway, starting with its passage over the most westerly flying junction in the kingdom, and confirming the sharpness of the curves which had affected the choice of motive power over the years. I might have missed the Adams' Radials, but at least I had a nodding acquaintance with one of their predecessors, the ex-L&SWR A1X 0-6-0T No. 734, known to me as No. 32646, which, with a sister engine, was bought from the LB&SCR by the L&SWR especially for use between Axminster and Lyme Regis.

Lyme Regis station was still pretty neat and tidy, and hosted a reasonable number of passengers. In the quiet between trains I wandered around the place, and was delighted to find a splendid working clock with "SWR" still emblazoned on its dial. There was also evidence that some member of station staff had a sense of humour. A notice of announcing 'Withdrawal of Railway Passenger Services' had been posted alongside a BR poster exhorting people to "get out and about this summer – by train" and urging those contemplating doing so to ask for details about offers from "this station".

In 1964 stations were still crowded with holidaymakers. Exeter St Davids, 5 September 1964. 'N' class 2-6-0 No. 31853 in charge of the 08.30 Padstow to Waterloo.

Above - No. 35022 'Holland-America Line' approaching Axminster with the 11.00 Waterloo - Ilfracombe express. The 'ACE'. 5 September 1964. I think this was the last time this train was steam-hauled.

Right - Just a few miles away at the terminus of the Lyme Regis branch from Axminster, there was somewhat of a contradiction in posters displayed.

Top left - WR single unit railcar No. W55019 leading a train of three such vehicles arriving at Lyme Regis with the 15.40 from Axminster. **Bottom -** Seen after arrival. **Top right -** The still extant - and working - SWR station clock at Lyme Regis by the well-known manufacturer of railway clocks, John Walker. All 5 September 1964.

Okehampton, 19 September 1964. No. 80064 entering the station to take up duty on a Padstow train.

During my earlier visit to Yeoford, I had met the redoubtable Peter W Gray, well known West Country railway photographer, intent upon the same mission as me. He enlisted me in the local branch of the Railway Correspondence and Travel Society, whose meetings I then regularly attended for the next couple of years or so. In the manner of such bodies, the RCTS networked with other like-minded organisations, and so it came about that a few of our members, of whom I was one, joined a gang from the Plymouth Railway Circle on a brake van trip over the Wenford Bridge branch.

This well-known freight only line was originally part of the ancient Bodmin and Wadebridge Railway, which was purchased – with somewhat dubious legality it has been claimed – by the L&SWR in 1847, but remained physically isolated from its parent company until 1895. As with the Lyme Regis branch, I was too late to witness the Southern steam locomotives which had worked it, in this case the long-lived and rather pretty Beattie well-tanks which had operated the line for many years, and which had made it famous, but at least on the occasion of my trip in mid-September 1965 it was still steam worked, but now by three ex-GWR 1366 class 0-6-0 panniers.

We were to join the train of brake vans at Wadebridge, and to get there we set sail from Exeter St Davids, and changed trains at Okehampton to one which would take us over "The Withered Arm" – the L&SWR's long meandering line

through North Cornwall which had eventually connected the Bodmin and Wadebridge to its other tracks. During the whole journey, although steam locomotives were extant, of ex-Southern locomotives, only one example, an N class 2-6-0, was seen at Okehampton. Aside from this there were only BR Standard Class 4 2-6-4Ts and Class 3 2-6-2Ts, and of course, the 1366s at Wadebridge.

This was my first and only return trip over what was once an important part of the Southern's system, and which was to be closed just over a year later. Halwill Junction, roughly in the middle of nowhere, was one of those places, of which there were a number in the British Isles, created by the arrival of the railway, subsequently becoming a settlement in its own right. Today its name remains, and I wonder how many of its present inhabitants realise that it was once a busy and important place where a main line and two branch lines met. As the train progressed from Okehampton, heading roughly north west, then roughly south-west, and then more or less west, I mentally christened the area served by the line 'the empty quarter' and, as we worked our way onwards around the northern slopes of Bodmin Moor, the scenery to the south became more austere, its desolation emphasised by a grey sky.

The sun began to peep through as we ran down into Wadebridge, and when the time came to climb aboard our brake vans it had turned into a pleasant enough day. I was delighted to find that included in the rake of vans was one of the Southern's bogie variety, No. S56278, and it was particularly agreeable that it was one those created by converting the redundant ex-LB&SCR overhead electric motor luggage vans in the early 1930's. These vehicles have been described as the most comfortable brake vans ever built in Britain. I believe that I opted to travel in it rather than one of the other vehicles.

The journey to Wenford Bridge was a real pleasure. Our train engine was 1369, and we trundled up the Camel Valley with her mellow exhaust beat at the front end. We paused a number of times *en route*. The first breather was on the Wenford side of Boscarne Junction where a tantalising track disappeared into an old shed which someone claimed housed an elderly platelayers' vehicle inside, but it was securely locked and we couldn't verify the claim. We then stopped prior to crossing the highway at Dunmere and then close by for a photo call in East Wood, where the sunlight dappled our train through the trees in this sylvan place. The next break was a leisurely one to take water from the ancient and curious device at Penhargard, and we then interrupted our progress to cross the lane at Hellandbridge and again at Tresarrett for another photo call.

Thus we eventually trundled into Wenford Bridge, where 1369 ran round the train of brake vans whilst their passengers made the most of the chance to wander about this rather remote seat of commerce. China clay was the principal traffic by a long way, but there were a few vans which had carried other goods scattered around. The rails which marked the beginning of the long-abandoned extension line which once connected Wenford Bridge to the De Lank Quarry by way of a cable-worked incline were still in place where it crossed the road next to the depot, after which the track bed disappeared under impenetrable undergrowth.

The return run, again with odd pauses and the watering stop, was just as enjoyable as the outward trip. When we eventually arrived back at Wadebridge, 1369 disposed of the brake vans, and before being put away for the day posed outside the locomotive shed with her two sisters. And then it was the train back to Exeter. As we returned through the empty quarter, I reflected that it had been an amazing day. It felt as though the trip to Wenford Bridge had put me almost directly in touch with a much earlier era of the railway business. I had been unbelievably fortunate.

Left - *En-route to Wadebridge. No. 80064 taking water at Launceston.*

Opposite top - *A pause in East Wood, Dunmere.*

Opposite bottom - *No. 1369 preparing to cross the lane at Hellandbridge with the 'Wenford Special'.*

All 19 September 1964.

Opposite page - *Water stop at Penhargard. The unusual water delivery device was known to railwaymen as 'The Spring'.*
Top - *Ex. SR bogie brake van, No. S56278, converted from LBSCR overhead electric luggage van, seen at Wenford Bridge.*
Bottom - *The Southern acquired five ex– West Coast joint Stock 12-wheel sleeping cars from the LMS to serve as staff dormitories. They were used during the summer season when extra men were required and were based at Lyme Regis, Seaton, Launceston, Bude and Wadebridge. This is the Wadebridge vehicle, No. DM198932.*

Top - *The end of the day at Wadebridge shed. No. 1369 joins her sisters, Nos. 1368 and 1367.*
Bottom - *Standard No. 82030 heads the 11.00 Padstow to Waterloo at Delabole. Both 19 September 1964.*

The next, and final, batch of memories comes from the next year, 1965. By this time it was clear that things were going rapidly down the route from which there could be no return. Steam was virtually extinct in the West Country, and a raft of line closures were happening or were due to happen. The latter were principally a result of the implementation of Dr Beeching's recommendations, and were to include a huge proportion of the Southern's network in the west. Before long, passengers would be eliminated on all the Southern lines west of Coleford Junction, with exception of the rump of the Callington branch. Closed to passengers, too, would be the line northwards from Halwill Junction to Torrington and onwards to Barnstaple, and most of the East Devon branches would have disappeared. In a matter of just a few years, of former Southern lines in Devon and Cornwall, only the downgraded main line from Exeter towards Waterloo, the Exmouth branch and the route from Exeter to Barnstaple and Ilfracombe would retain passenger services, and even the Barnstaple to Ilfracombe provision would be knocked on the head in 1970.

My interest could adapt to the changing times, albeit with sadness, but it became a priority to track down remnants of the old order where and when I could, and 1965 I had a few excursions which gave something of a flavour of how things once were.

Another of my wheels turned the full circle in June. The local RCTS branch organised a trip to Eastleigh, now in its final phase as a works catering for steam locomotives. We travelled from Exeter to Salisbury, where the change was made to a Hampshire diesel for the remainder of the journey. It was good to be back in a land where steam was still around, even if it was only part of the total scene.

Eastleigh works had been altered a little since my previous visit in 1958. The tenants were much more diverse in terms of origin, there was a dedicated space for dealing with diesels, and steam and electric traction mingled in the erecting shop. The mingling was evidenced by London Transport ex-GW 0-6-0PT No. L94 sitting happily alongside electro-diesel Bo-Bo No. E6005, and by the presence of electric locomotives Bo-Bo No. E5011 and ex-Southern Raworth-Bulleid Co-Co No. 20003 surrounded by Light Pacifics and Standard Class 5 4-6-0s.

In the steaming shed were another Standard Class 5, No. 75041, and Ivatt Class 4MT 2-6-0, both in brilliant condition, giving an impression of a glimmer of hope for steam.

Looking south from Campbell Road bridge at Eastleigh (most views are in the other direction), No. 34019 'Bideford approaches the station with an up Bournemouth line working. The access and exit lines from the shed are on the left. 12 June 1965.

Eastleigh Works, 12 June 1965.

Opposite top - Bo-Bo electric locomotive E5011 in the erecting shop.

Opposite bottom - London Transport 5700, No. L94 undergoing overhaul.

Right - A first series Electro-Diesel, No. E6005.

Bottom - Raworth-Bulleid CC Co-Co, No. 20003 and WC No. 34098 'Templecombe'. All 12 June 1965.

Next two pages:

Top left - Nos. 34098 and 34088.

Bottom left - Quietness and serenity (temporarily - well it was Saturday) in the boiler shop.

Top right - M7. No 30053 set aside for preservation'

Bottom right - No. 30926 'Repton' stored pending preservation. All 12 June 1965.

Eastleigh Motive Power Depot, 12 June 1964.
Top - *One of the last 'Q' 0-6-0's, No. 30548, minus coupling rods, awaits scrapping.*
Bottom - *At the rear of the shed a similar fate awaited ''U' class 2-6-0, No. 31620.*

A visitor for the Fawley oil trains, 9F No. 92153 and No. 34103 'Calstock' outside the rear of the shed.

Another faint glimmer was provided by the presence outside the works of 'Schools' class 4-4-0 No. 30926 *Repton* and M7 class 0-4-4T No. 30053, both looking somewhat down-at-heel, but happily awaiting preservation.

From the works we progressed to the motive power depot, where the first, and most agreeable, sighting was USA No. 30064 acting as shed pilot, but, aside from her, of Southern types in service there were merely three Light Pacifics and S15 No. 30824. Also scattered around were a number of Standard machines, including 9F 2-10-0 No. 92153, and Stanier Class 8F 2-8-0 No. 48408 was also present. As ever, there was a line of dead locomotives, amongst which were two other ex-Southern engines – U class 2-6-0 No. 31620 and one of the very last Q 0-6-0s, No. 30548, both minus motion and coupling rods.

The visit made an interesting enough event, but the inevitability of the end of the era covered the day with something of a blanket of despondency. The same can also be said for my next jaunt to the Southern in August, when the local RCTS devised another tour, this time to Bournemouth and Weymouth sheds.

Again we travelled the Southern main line, this time as far as Yeovil Junction, where we took the rail-bus which ran round the houses to Yeovil Town and thence by reversal to Yeovil Pen Mill station. It is a sobering thought that the whole of this old network of connecting railways has gone and that there is now little evidence that it once existed. Yeovil Town GW shed was empty except for a handful of dead locomotives, and was clearly near the end. From Pen Mill we journeyed down the Great Western line to Weymouth, where "Merchant Navy" and Light Pacifics were on show, and from there on Southern metals to Bournemouth.

Bournemouth and Weymouth sheds were further witnesses to the run-down of steam. Abandoned and dead engines abounded, there were piles of ashes and clinker which in former times would have been cleared, and the places were rather dishevelled and untidy. One was left in no doubt that a winding down process was advancing rapidly. The only saving grace was that there *were* still steam engines around, and that they *were*, while they lasted, still making a good show. Some were even quite clean!

Curiously, the next excursion was not so discouraging. I'm

Top - No. 34005 'Barnstaple' with empty tank cars passes through Eastleigh en route for Fawley. The engine will be removed from the train before the final passage down the Fawley branch itself.

Bottom - No. 34082 '615 Squadron' with an up Waterloo express at Eastleigh. On the left, a Hampshire diesel unit leaves Platform 4 for Fareham and Portsmouth via Botley. Portsmouth via Botley.   Both 12 June 1965.

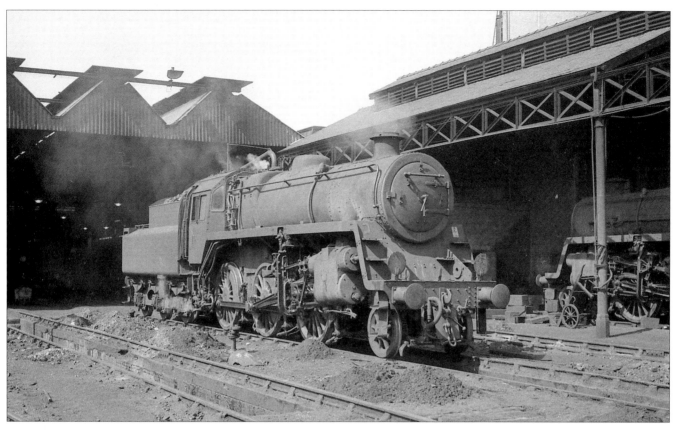

Top - *Standard class 4 No. 76015 on shed at Bournemouth.*
Bottom - *Ivatt class 2 2-6-2T No. 41293 'dead' at Weymouth MPD.*
Both 14 August 1965.

Weymouth arrival and departure.

Right - *No. 34053 'Sir Keith Park' arriving with the 13.30 Waterloo - Weymouth.*

Above - *No. 35017 'Belgian Marine' leaving with the 17.35 Weymouth to Waterloo.*

Both 14 August 1965.

Top - Line up of power at Weymouth. L to R: West Country No. 34101 'Hartland', Merchant navy No. 35005 'Canadian Pacific', Grange class No. 6870 'Bodicote Grange' and Ivatt Class 2 No. 41293.
Bottom - Bulleid Pacific driving and pony truck wheels at Weymouth.
Both 14 August 1965.

not absolutely certain why, but maybe it was because it was a final visit to total steam country. In any case, it was the turning of the full circle of my final wheel.

Whilst I had been exiled in East Anglia, my employers there had acquired the Eclipse Peat Company, which extracted sedge peat from the fields around Ashcott in Somerset. In these days of conservation this is considered a most politically incorrect activity, but at that time it was a flourishing industry, and Eclipse Peat, in common with many other organisations in the same business elsewhere, used an extensive system of narrow gauge railways to transport the peat from fields to the processing plant. I had known the Managing Director of Eclipse Peat from my East Anglian days, and secured his authorisation for an RCTS visit, which happened towards the end of October.

To get to Ashcott, we took the GW main line from Devon to Highbridge, and from there used the Somerset and Dorset. The latter was by now part of fiefdom of the Western Region, which had never particularly wanted it and was making every effort to get rid of it, but somewhat amusingly the S & D, totally populated by steam engines, rather spoiled the Western's promise of eliminating steam from its territory by the end of 1965 by having a lingering passenger service until 1966.

Highbridge station still had the flat crossing where the S & D ran over the Bristol to Taunton main line to access freight facilities, and in addition to the two platforms serving the GW there were a further four serving the needs of the S & D, by now a massive over-provision, two for through traffic to Burnham on Sea — no longer running — and two for terminating trains. A distant view of the remains of the S & D works added some more interest. The Highbridge – Evercreech Junction section was served by Ivatt Class 2 2-6-2Ts, and one of these brought us to Ashcott, where a short walk took us to the Eclipse Peat Works. A most engaging few hours ensued as we were transported around the 2' 0" gauge system in empty peat wagons drawn by a Lister petrol locomotive (Maker's No. 25366). It was all great fun. At one point the Eclipse Peat system crossed the S & D on the level, and every time a narrow gauge train made the crossing, telephone permission had to be sought for the transit, presumably from Shapwick and Glastonbury.

After the visit to the peat fields, we travelled to Evercreech and Templecombe, savouring the last of the S & D. On the return trip, I stopped off at Edington. The wheel had indeed turned full circle. By this time, of course, Edington had long ceased to be a junction, assuming the name "Edington Burtle", and was a mere shadow of what it had once been. All traces of the Bridgwater branch had long gone, but there were hints of former times, including an LSW mile post indicating "0", apparently marking the point where it left the line to Burnham.

My final memory of the Southern in this era is of a trip,

Highbridge for Burnham on Sea, with No. 41206 (last seen on the Callington branch) heading a train for Evercreech Junction. 23 October 1965.

Moods of the S & D. No. 41290 moving on shed at Highbridge after having brought in a train from Evercreech Junction. 23 October 1965.

PASSENGERS ARE REQUESTED TO CROSS THE LINE BY THE BRIDGE

The famed flat crossing at Highbridge where the S & D line to Burnham on Sea intersected the GWR Bristol - Exeter route. Note the distinctive shape of the signal box. 23 October 1965.

Above and bottom left: The flat crossing where the Eclipse Peat Company's two foot gauge line crossed the S & D Highbridge branch . and the S & D Highbridge branch. The passengers on the narrow gauge train are from the RCTS. Motive power is provided by Lister locomotive, maker's No. 25366.

Top left - The driver of the Lister locomotive telephones BR for permission to cross the line.

Bottom row - S & D relics. L to R: Trespass Notice at Ashcott, Fire bucket notice and the bottom of the dreaded closure notice, also at Ashcott and Gradient post at Edington Burtle with LSW '0' milepost for the long-gone Bridgewater branch. 23 October 1965.

All 23 October 1965.

Views of the Eclipse Peat Company's System

Top - *Road vehicles transported the peat from this unloading bank across the main road to the works.*

Bottom - *Permanent way maintenance gang returning from the peat fields to their base.*

Right - *Three way point and wagons at the peat works. As interesting approach to curves!*　　　*All 23 October 1965.*

again with the RCTS, to Meldon Quarry, long time supplier of ballast to the LSWR and its successors. It was at the end of the first week in December, and, goodness, it was cold and windy. We alighted from a train for Bude at Meldon Platform, normally only used by quarry workers, into the teeth of a bitter north-easterly which made its presence felt throughout the whole visit. This was at the time when the rail access to the quarry was only by reversal from the main line, which meant that all trains into and out of the workings had to use Meldon Viaduct. The latter is a pretty, spindly steel trestle, and is still in use today as a cycle track and footpath. An observed little jewel nearby was an L&SWR boundary marker. We looked at strata, crushers, wagons

and other pieces of equipment, and, *pièce de résistance*, sheltering from the wind in her tiny shed, the quarry shunter, USA 0-6-0T DS234, formerly 30062. At the time of our visit, she was the last British Rail steam locomotive west of Exeter.

The tour finished, and, frozen by the wind, we were glad to board a warm train from Bude at Meldon Platform for the return to Exeter. I remember that my face was immoveable because of being screwed up to cope with the cold. It was like a temporary attack of Bell's palsy, and I had only just about unfrozen when we reached our destination.

Above - Melton Platform, used by quarry workers (and visiting RCTS members). A train from Plymouth is approaching.

Right - LSWR boundary post at Meldon Quarry.

Opposite top and bottom - Meldon Quarry.

Centre left - Just beyond the quarry, Meldon Viaduct, seen from the south.

Centre right - The last BR steam engine to operate in Devon. USA No. DS234 in the quarry shed.

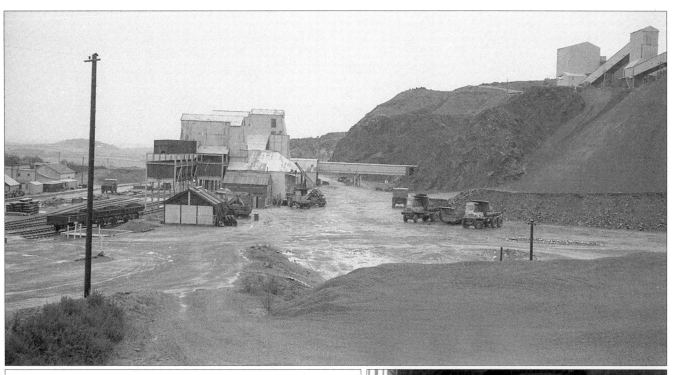

Epilogue

It seems to me that the sighting of the last British Rail steam locomotive in the south west peninsula, and the recollection of bitter mid-winter cold might perhaps make this an appropriate place to wind up my memoir.

If the final sections have seemed to have been written by a slightly dismal pen, it is simply a reflection of how things were as I remember them. I had to move with the changing times, of course, and certainly accepted that many things that the new era brought with it were both positive and necessary, and sometimes even pleasing. This, however, could not mean that I would part willingly with what I had grown up with, and had loved. The days that I have described in

this work, particularly in the earlier parts, were somehow the days of more certainty. Railways, main line or minor branch, were the thread which joined the fabric of our lives together, and the steam locomotives which ran on them seemed mankind's most stirring creation.

And because I was surrounded by it for so many of my younger years, the old Southern, before and after nationalisation, was the part of the railway that I loved the best. It is because of my love that I have tried to describe in this book the Southern scenes that my mind projects upon the screen of remembrance. In doing so, I hope that I might have enabled the reader to share some of my past pleasures.

Opposite top - WC class No. 34107 'Blandford Forum' arrives at Broad Clyst with the 15.34 all stations Templecombe to Exeter Central. 8 August 1964.

Opposite bottom - BB 4-6-2 No. 34059 'Sir Archibald Sinclair' brings an Exeter Central - Templecombe stopping train into Sidmouth Junction. 6 September 1963.

Right - Full circle. My first remembered train trip was from Edington Junction in 1944. I travelled from the same station again (although it had by now been re-christened Edington Burtle after the closure of the Bridgwater branch) on 23 October 1965, also the occasion of my last journey on a regular service steam-hauled train. This is the working before my finale. Ivatt Class 2 2-6-2T No. 41291 leaves with a train for Highbridge.

Top - *Small country town station. Ottery St Mary waits in the sunshine for custom The line of barrows points, perhaps, to busier times.*

Bottom - *Opened by the Southern Region in 1955, the modern signal box at Ottery St Mary was destined to have a life of just less than 12 years.* *Both 29 August 1964.*

Top - *Ivatt Class 2 No. 41322 at Exmouth with a train for Tipton St johns, 6 September 1963.*

Right - *An unexpected piece of railway history. The former London and South Western Railway receiving office 'for goods and parcels to all parts', Sutton Harbour, Plymouth, still clearly labelled in August 1965.*

Top - The classic view of Seaton Junction. No. 34070 'Manston' leaving with the 15.35 Exeter Central to Salisbury stopping service. 11 July 1964.

Bottom - No. 34096 'Trevone' arriving at Axminster with the 13.45 Yeovil Junction - Seaton Junction service. 5 September 1964.

Top - Exeter Central, 2 May 1964. West Country No. 34002 'Salisbury' with a train for North Devon, with 57xx 0-6-0PT No. 3759 on banking duties.
Bottom - No. 34070 'Manston' leaving Exeter St Davids with a Plymouth, via Okehampton, train. 7 September 1963.

The end of the line. Z class 0-8-0T No. 30951 awaits her fate in the scrap line at Exeter St Davids. 7 September 1963.